tor:

Ell *ining)*

Ellie is no stran(
a magical myna
delivers an invitation to a mysterious gathering,
Ellie takes it all in her stride. This, she hopes will
be the start of her training and the beginning of
her search to find the lost Earth Witches. But is
she really prepared for the adventure? Will she
be strong enough to overcome the dangers that
lie ahead and will she learn to control her newly
found powers?

Finalist - Children's/Juvenile Early Readers/Chapter
Books (Fiction) category Next Generation Indie Book
Awards 2022

Bryony Fairview: Weather Witch

A book about magic, adventure, courage and
friendship where two newly found friends try to
save both their lands (and the world!) from the
wild storms that are coming. When Ellie finds a
very upset and grumpy Weather Witch called
Bryony in her garden, she is eager to find out
why she is there and what her problem is. Little
does Ellie know how deeply involved she will
become in Bryony's world and how the meeting will eventually lead to a
secret buried deep within her own past.

Inspiration can come from anywhere. For this story, I delved into my family tree and added a sprinkle of the mythology I adored as a child. My family is a vibrant tapestry of characters — my grandparents and their grandparents journeyed from places like India, Germany, France, England, and Wales, bringing with them their tales of adventure. These stories have been passed down through generations, and they made my childhood feel like pure magic.

As I grew up, I was delighted to begin weaving my own stories and adventures. Those adventures eventually led me to one of the most magical places in the world — Ireland. Here, with my young family, we immerse ourselves in the rich myths and fae folklore of this mystical island.

Throughout *'The Legend of Dragonfoot'*, you'll find nods to my family, both past and present, as well as hints of the mythology and folklore that have always inspired me. Magic is all around us — and I hope this story helps you see it too.

The Legend of Dragonfoot

Written by
Rebecca Burke

Illustrated by
Chris Burke

REBECCA BURKE – Author
Though Rebecca's background is more science based, having studied
Sports Therapy and worked with the young physically disabled, she has
always had a very big imagination and love for faery folklore and nature.
When Rebecca relocated to Ireland she was able to let her imagination run
wild and when her two daughters were born they became her inspiration
for writing children's books.

CHRIS BURKE – Illustrator
After a lifetime of service, initially in the Defence Forces and then in the
Civil Service, Chris discovered his creative side in retirement. He had had
his artwork displayed in several exhibitions. As a grandfather, he has
thoroughly enjoyed channelling the magic of his grandchildren into his
illustrations.

First published in 2025 by Child's Eye,
Redshank Books

Copyright © Rebecca Burke and Chris Burke

The right of Rebecca Burke and Chris Burke
to be identified as the authors of this work
has been asserted in accordance with the
Copyright, Designs and Patents Act, 1988.

ISBN 978-1-912969-81-4

A CIP catalogue record for this book is
available from The British Library

Cover and design by Carnegie Book Production

Redshank Books
Brunel House
Volunteer Way
Faringdon
Oxfordshire
SN7 7YR

Tel: +44 (0)845 873 3837

www.libripublishing.co.uk

Dedication:

Dedicated to all of the Dragonfoot descendants

The Legend of Dragonfoot –

They say legends are created under a full moon – and the
moon was especially full the night this story began. But not
all legends start with a prophecy. Some begin by accident, like
Dragonfoot. Dragonfoot, a young and unassuming creature,
unwittingly becomes the guardian of the most magical
treasure in all the worlds: the last Dragon's egg. What follows
is a thrilling journey which takes him through hidden worlds
filled with enchantment, danger, and mystery. Along the way,
he learns the value of trust, the courage to face his fears, and
the true power of knowing his own worth.

Chapter 1

The Find

Legends, they say, are created under a
full moon and the moon was particularly
full the night our story begins. You see,
some legends are born to be, some grow
up knowing they will become legends and
then, there was this little one who found himself
curled up and scared, in a thorny bush. He did not
know how he came to be in this bush and did not
know where he had come from - all he knew was he
was hungry and alone. His name was Dragonfoot.

As dawn approached, he heard an angry muttering,
and some heavy footsteps getting closer and closer. He
drew his knees to his chest and hugged them tightly as

the bush's brambles were pushed apart and the light of dawn flooded through onto him. Once his eyes had adjusted to the light, he could see the figure that stood above him. He had expected an angry goblin or ogre but instead there was this large, scaly creature with a broad smile on its face and glasses perched on a small snout-like nose, similar to that of a lizard or a dragon.

'You're too big for a fairy and too small to be a dragon, what are you I wonder?' The creature spoke with a soft, curious, voice as it reached into the bush grabbing Dragonfoot by the scruff of his neck and lifting him swiftly out of the brambles. It walked around him pondering out loud, 'You're not very scaled... no... there's an odd mark on your leg and that foot is positively dinky! Yet that one...... now that one looks familiar!' The creature chuckled as it stuck out its own foot and wiggled its clawed toes showing Dragonfoot that it looked like his.

'I'm Bea, I'm part of the Dragonfeet tribe here in Draig.' She spoke puffing out her chest proudly. 'Do you have a name?'

Dragonfoot stood up slowly as a slight shiver ran through him. Bea chuckled again. Composing himself he shyly spoke, 'I am Dragonfoot.' Bea burst out laughing, rolling onto her back holding her tummy. Dragonfoot just stood there and watched as she rolled around.

He blushed but continued slightly louder – 'I don't know how I got here and I don't know where I came from.' By this point Bea had stopped laughing and had a serious look on her face.

'No idea at all?' she asked, concerned. Dragonfoot shook his head. 'Hmmm, that is a conundrum. I'll take you back to the elders, they'll have the answer.' She turned to look over to a valley in the distance., 'Can you fly?' she asked.

'I don't think so,' Dragonfoot replied shocked.

'I suppose you would only have the one wing, seeing as you only have the one dragon foot.' Bea was talking absolute nonsense from what Dragonfoot could see.

'Can *you* fly?' he asked her and without hesitation she replied 'Of course! We're not called the Dragonfeet tribe for *just* our feet, they're just where the magic happens.' She smiled broadly again as Dragonfoot tried to make sense of what she was saying.

Bea didn't want to waste any time, she was far too excited about her *find* and wanted to show him off to the rest of the tribe. She was sure it would put Seren, her cousin's, nose out of joint as *he*

had only discovered an Oak tree whereas *she* had just discovered a whole new species!

'Quick I'll show you, climb onto my back and hold on tightly!' Dragonfoot did what she said, not really knowing what was about to happen.

Bea started to stamp her large, clawed feet, dust flying up from the dry ground. She stamped them faster and faster, until sparks flew around them. Suddenly she began to grow larger, her scales shimmered in the light and enormous beautiful wings sprouted out of her back. Dragonfoot held on as tightly as he could as she flew up into the air and soared towards the valley.

Within no time they were landing in a bustling valley with music and sweet smells filling the air. Dragonfoot jumped off Bea as she transformed back.

'You became a dragon!' He spoke with absolute wonder.

She smiled. 'Not really a dragon, but a dragon-like creature. Dragons are far bigger than we could ever become'. Bea reached out her hand and grabbed Dragonfoot. 'Quick, let me take you to the elders.'

Bea was hopping with excitement, yet Dragonfoot was a little nervous as they arrived at a cave embedded in the bank.

'This is the home of the elders, there's no need to be nervous, come on' Bea said softly as she led him inside.

To his surprise the cave was not pitch black. Instead, a warm glow filled the entrance lighting up clearly the several tunnels that lay before them. Without hesitation Bea walked down the central one, Dragonfoot in tow.

The tunnel, though narrow to start with had already begun to broaden out, leading them to a *ginormous* room that sparkled. Each wall was lined with piles of gold and precious stones, sparkling with blues and reds. In the centre of the room was a large, sleeping dragon of red and gold, curled around a large iridescent, scaled, egg. Dragonfoot stumbled back and covered his mouth to muffle the scream he felt coming.

Bea chuckled her chuckle 'Nothing will wake her, she sleeps very soundly, and is generally harmless – as long as we don't touch her egg that is.'

Dragonfoot sighed with relief as he let his hand drop back down to his side. They continued through this room and into another tunnel which was much longer and narrower than the others. Eventually

they entered a room where ten, hunched figures sat around a large oval table with a much younger one stood up at the back of the room.

'What are you doing here?'

Bea called out, annoyed at the standing figure. It just smirked at Bea and she stuck her tongue out at him – it was Seren her cousin.

'I was summoned by the elders, like all the important tribe members are,' Seren replied in a condescending manner.

Bea screwed up her hands to fists and stamped her foot, forgetting where she was for a second. As she remembered she straightened herself up and spoke to the figures that were sat around the table.

'Elders I wish to show you my find from today. I expect you will be more than impressed. I would say it was the most unique find of our tribe... ever.' With the last word she shot a look at Seren and sneakily stuck her tongue out again at him.

Dragonfoot wasn't sure how he felt about being called a 'find', but was too nervous to say anything so remained quiet.

The elders slowly turned to look at Bea.

'This had better be good Bea, we don't have time for your silliness today,' one particularly grumpy and wrinkled elder said. Bea blushed and clearing her throat she nervously replied, 'It is.'

'Then show us what it is - this find you speak of?' another snapped.

Dragonfoot wished he was anywhere else but here They were so grumpy. As this thought filled his head, he suddenly felt himself being lifted up by the ankle. Bea held Dragonfoot high in the air showing the elders the strange marking on his leg

'Look,' she said, 'an ancient marking on his tiny leg and look at this foot.' She grabbed his other ankle, 'He has a dragon foot.'

'The mark of The Beforan' one elder said to another, 'and so young.' Another spoke 'You don't suppose it could be...' The elders muttered excitedly amongst themselves. It was Seren who blushed now, in anger. Bea's find was very unique.

Bea, still holding Dragonfoot upside down, grew with confidence and stood even taller showing off her find. 'He is called Dragonfoot.'

Seren smirked.

'It was the name he came with!' Bea indignantly retorted, while lowering Dragonfoot to the ground, 'I would've chosen something much less literal'.

Dragonfoot sat on the ground and looked down at the mark on his leg, tracing it's outline gently with his finger, wishing it would trigger a memory. 'The Beforan' he had heard one of the elders say, but what was The Beforan? Before he could ask his question aloud one of the elders was towering over him. He was so large and wrinkled, he could barely open his eyes. Dragonfoot gulped loudly as he stood himself up. Then the elder smiled at him, not as invitingly as Bea's broad smile, but it eased the fear a little.

'Walk with me child' the elder gestured to Dragonfoot to walk beside him.

They walked back through the tunnels and out into the broad daylight. The valley was beautiful and the air so sweet. Dragonfoot took a deep breath in and exhaled with a smile.

'Do you speak?' The elder asked, looking at Dragonfoot inquisitively.

'Yes,' Dragonfoot croaked, then clearing his throat he continued 'yes I speak well, I think, but I don't know where I have come from, I don't know what the markings mean and I can't fly' he spoke so fast he stumbled a little on the words. He wasn't sure if this was due to his nerves, him being hungry or him wanting answers, either way the elder chuckled a little.

'That is a lot of information you have given me,' he smiled and walked on a little more, 'but first shall we have breakfast?'

Dragonfoot, thrown a little by the question, looked ahead and realised they were coming to a small entrance in another part of the bank and the smells coming out were mouth-wateringly good! The elder tapped on the door gently with one of his long-clawed fingers, almost immediately chains and bolts could be heard unlocking. The door opened wide and there in the doorway stood a little pixie. She had a purple apron on and had flour in her hair.

'What has your Ash Bird sourced for breakfast today, Maple?' The elder asked the pixie as he leant down to her level.

'Everything! She's had a wonderful harvest - nuts, berries and even some honeycomb! She's even had to fly back out as she couldn't carry it all in one go.'

The elder nodded, impressed with the answer. It was then that Dragonfoot's stomach growled with hunger, so loudly it made Maple jump.

'Oh, that is a very hungry tummy,' she said turning and rushing back through the door, 'Sit! Sit!' she called ''shan't be long, a feast you shall have!'

As Dragonfoot and the elder sat down on a grassy mound a beautiful bird flew overhead. Its wings spanned out showing all its multi-coloured feathers in full glory and in its talons was an array of fruits and vegetables.

'So that is the Ash Bird,' Dragonfoot thought to himself as the bird gently landed and scurried through the little door. Almost as soon as the bird went in Maple was rushing out with two plates full of tasty treats. Dragonfoot's eyes grew so big, the elder and Maple smiled. 'Eat, no need to wait. Your tummy won't be happy until you're fed.' Maple gestured to Dragonfoot with her hands to eat the food. He didn't hesitate for long and tucked into the feast, barely looking up until his plate was empty. The elder smiled as he slowly sipped his drink.

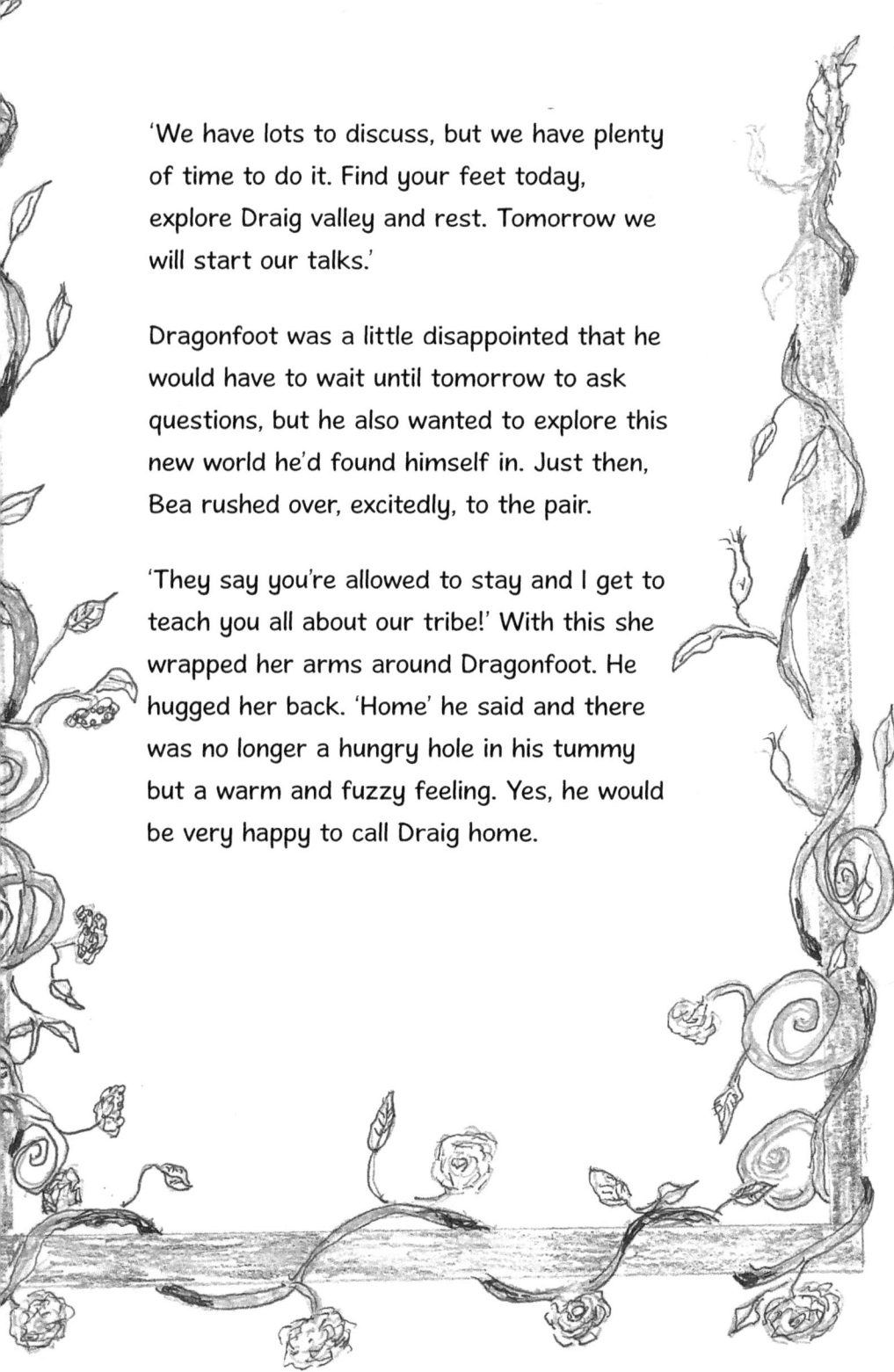

'We have lots to discuss, but we have plenty of time to do it. Find your feet today, explore Draig valley and rest. Tomorrow we will start our talks.'

Dragonfoot was a little disappointed that he would have to wait until tomorrow to ask questions, but he also wanted to explore this new world he'd found himself in. Just then, Bea rushed over, excitedly, to the pair.

'They say you're allowed to stay and I get to teach you all about our tribe!' With this she wrapped her arms around Dragonfoot. He hugged her back. 'Home' he said and there was no longer a hungry hole in his tummy but a warm and fuzzy feeling. Yes, he would be very happy to call Draig home.

Chapter 2

The Dragon's Song

Bea was buzzing with excitement. She couldn't wait to start showing Dragonfoot all the amazing things the Dragonfeet tribe did and she was intrigued to see what magic, if any, she would be able to teach him.

'Come with me,' she said grabbing Dragonfoot's arm. The elder coughed indicating to Bea to be polite. Blushing she then added 'If you are full and ready that is.' Dragonfoot was and he couldn't wait to explore, he nodded excitedly and hopped to his feet. Off they walked arm in arm Bea happily chatting away.

'So, the Dragonfeet Tribe are the oldest creatures here in Draig' Bea was saying, 'and it's our duty to discover and name things! Though that hasn't happened for a long while as most things have already been found and named, that is until I found you... Although you did already have a name... But you still count!' She barely stopped to take a breath as she continued, 'so now we protect all the creatures, though I'm not really sure what from, but we are always practicing and perfecting our magic for the time we will need it!'

'Do you ever use your magic for fun?' Dragonfoot asked as Bea paused for a second, she stopped and looked at him,

'Well, we're not supposed to but sometimes I can't help myself. But only little magic spells, like changing the colour of objects, that sort of thing.' Dragonfoot's eyes widened.

'Can you teach me to do that?' he asked. Bea nodded.

'I'll have to! I mean I am now in charge of your training so I will have to start from the very beginning, it's only right you know.' They took a few more steps and were then on top of a hill covered in tiny white flowers.

'Here we are,' she said and turned to face Dragonfoot. 'This is heather, my sister named it, she loves white flowers but hates pink... Watch this!' She stamped her feet gently and then began to dance through the flowers, as the sparks from her feet touched the white flowers they began to change to shades of pink. She danced until she'd shaped a large B in pink flowers among the white, then chuckling her chuckle she flopped down on the ground by Dragonfoot.

'How did you do that?' he asked,

'It's easy,' Bea replied 'just
gently tap your clawed foot,
I doubt you have any magic in
your tiny one, and then think
really hard about the colour
you want the flowers to become. Once your foot
begins to spark then that's the magic working!'

'Sounds easy enough,' Dragonfoot thought to himself
as he started to tap his clawed foot on the ground.

'Not tap, stamp... but gently!' snapped Bea quickly at him.

'What is the difference between a tap and a gentle stamp?'
Dragonfoot said in his head as he tried again, this time a little
harder. His foot tingled, he stamped again, it almost felt like it
was fizzing and then, on the next stamp, there were positively
sparks flying from it. With a hop and a skip and a few more
stamps he began to dance around in the white flowers of
the heather. Bea watched with pride as his foot touched the
delicate flowers changing each one to different shades of
purples, pinks and reds.

Dragonfoot ran now, up and down the hillside, hopping,
skipping, giggling — he didn't want to stop! Bea joined in with
his dance and before long there wasn't a single white flower
on the hillside. As they spun, they accidently kicked each
other's foot, a big blue spark flew out from the knock. Both

creatures stopped and looked at the patch where the spark landed.

'Blue!' Bea squealed 'We changed them to blue!' Both creatures giggled and lay down in the colourful flowers, exhausted and happy.

They lay on their backs and looked up to the sky for a while in silence. The day was already nearly over as dusk started to envelop the hill.

I'Listen,' Bea suddenly said, 'can you hear that?'

Dragonfoot listened carefully, his ears twitching a little, then he heard a very faint sound. It sounded like a tune floating through the air.

'Yes,' he said excitedly, 'yes I hear it — what is it?'

Bea gave a broad smile. 'It's the Dragon's Song. Look over there.' She pointed up to the sky in the direction where the sun was setting. The tune became louder and louder as dragons of all colours flew right over their heads. Bea stretched her arms up to the sky and spread out her fingers.

'This is my favourite part of the day!' She had to shout as the beautiful melody had gotten so loud! Dragonfoot watched mesmerised at the beautiful creatures - who knew such *ginormous* creatures could glide so effortlessly through the sky. It was while watching as the wind trickled over and under the dragons' wings that Dragonfoot figured out how the music was made. Silence fell again on the hillside as the last of the dragons flew overhead and vanished into the distance.

Bea sighed, 'It used to last much longer, there are so few dragons now.' She seemed lost in thought for a moment then suddenly jumped up to her feet, 'We must be getting back, the elders will start to worry!' She offered Dragonfoot a hand up. The friends giggled and danced the whole way back to the valley, neither noticing the small sparks flying off Dragonfoot's clawed foot. One spark landed on a moth that was resting on a plant. As soon as the spark touched the moth both the plant and it vanished.

The valley was much quieter as the friends arrived back, most creatures had gone home for the evening - in fact the only creatures that were still out were three of the ten elders who were patiently waiting for Bea and Dragonfoot to return.

'Sorry we lost track of time,' Bea explained catching her breath. The elders remained silent and motioned to the friends to follow them. They followed them back to the entrance of the elders' cave,

One elder turned and spoke as the other two hobbled into their cave, 'Camp in together tonight, tomorrow your own room will be carved out.' Bea and Dragonfoot nodded and waited for the last elder to go before Bea dragged Dragonfoot to her room.

All the tribe slept in different burrows all sprouting from the one cave, 'for safety', Bea had explained. The carved-out burrows were small but beautiful, as the different gems of the cave poked through adding flecks of colour here and there. Bea's room was mainly purple from the amethysts that were found in her part of the cave, her bed was carved directly into the rock. 'You can bunk there tonight,' she said pointing over at a pile of smooth rocks, 'should be plenty soft enough.' To Dragonfoot's surprise she was right. The stones felt good under his back, smooth and cool, in no time he was in a deep sleep.

The next morning Bea was up bright and early singing jolly songs about fairies and witches of the sky and earth. Dragonfoot yawned and stretched out his arms and legs almost falling off his bed of rocks. Jumping to his feet he was ready for the day. Bea handed him a belt from which many pockets dangled.

'Here, I made this for you last night — my own design - I call it a belt bag.' Bea loved to invent useful things, her most favourite invention were her glasses but this one was a very close second! 'You'll find it is perfect to store any curiosities you may find. Oh, and here,' she said passing him a packed lunch and a bottle of water. 'Today we explore more so we must be prepared!' she said eagerly placing her bag belt on. Dragonfoot put his lunch and water in one of the many pockets, he smiled as they fitted perfectly, then the two friends headed out of the cave to discover more of Draig.

At the entrance of the cave an elder sat hunched on a stool, leaning forward onto his gnarly walking stick. As the friends went to pass him, he grabbed Dragonfoot by the scruff of his neck. 'Uh uh uh,' he tutted 'today you learn about the Beforan. Only when you know where you have come from can you truly learn where you are going to.' Bea, noticeably disappointed, huffed.

'Will it take long?' she sulked, suddenly straightening up as she remembered who she was addressing.

'It will take as long as it needs to' the elder snapped back at her. Blushing, Bea scurried back into the cave, holding back tears.

'Come.' The elder ordered Dragonfoot to walk with him leaning on his shoulder as he hobbled through the valley.

'You remember nothing?' the elder quizzed, Dragonfoot shook his head, 'Do you know what the mark on your leg means?'

Shyly Dragonfoot spoke 'I heard it means The Beforan, but I do not know what that means. Do you suppose I was born with it?'

'My child, I don't suppose anything. I know that that is not the case. It is a mark not from birth but from travel.' They continued to stroll through the valley as they spoke.

'Do you have any marks from travel?' Dragonfoot asked. The elder shook his head.

'I've travelled this world that is true, but the travel mark you possess does not mark just any travel. It marks a travel through magic means to whole different worlds. I wish to know if it was from your own magic or if there was another who travelled with you.'

Dragonfoot's head spun. He desperately tried to remember something and make sense of it all. Surely, he couldn't have

travelled magically by himself, for it was only yesterday he learnt he could do any magic at all let alone *that* amount!

'You,' the elder continued, 'you could possibly be one of the most magical beings we have had here in Draig – potentially in all the worlds!' He chuckled a croaky chuckle, 'But you are so young and untrained it would seem, how could you be such a creature?' Although it was phrased like a question the elder did not want an answer. It was a statement, hanging in the air as he pondered about how to continue.

'Bea said she found you huddled in a bramble bush.' Dragonfoot nodded as the elder continued, 'but it is not your average bramble bush, no. It was a blue-thorned bramble bush.' The elder paused and looked at Dragonfoot. Seeing the lost look on his face, the elder explained, 'There have not been any blue-thorned bramble bushes for many, many, years. They have been thought to be extinct, yet there you were, found in a sizeable one just yesterday. One that was not there the day before and not only that but you also bear the mark of The Beforan, a *world* that is long lost.'

Dragonfoot looked up at the elder. 'But how?' he muttered.

'That is what I aim to find out today,' the elder said and with that he dragged Dragonfoot under a large tree. The magnificent leaves sheltered the pair from the sun that beamed down on Draig Valley. The elder stood staring at Dragonfoot as if to read his thoughts. Dragonfoot was uncomfortable with this and tried to cast his eyes anywhere else rather than at the wrinkled little eyes glaring at him. As he glanced to the ground, he studied his foot and the elder's.

'Could I possibly, actually, be one of you? One of the Dragonfeet tribe I mean. We have the same feet... well foot' He realised he was just babbling out whatever thought came to his mind and yet he could not stop. 'Last night I had the strangest dream, I was flying on Bea's back with all the dragons beside us, we seemed to be flying away from something but then the moon turned blue...'

'And that is why you are absolutely not one of us.' The elder almost spat out his words. Dragonfoot, mid-sentence, stopped immediately, mouth open, frozen.

'We, the Dragonfeet Tribe do not dream. Ever.' It was almost as if 'dream' was a bad word. Dragonfoot did not know how to respond, for *his* dream was so vivid last night - and nice.

'Why?' he finally spoke almost in a whisper afraid he would anger the elder.

'No time, no need' the elder replied as he gazed away from Dragonfoot and beyond the valley.

'How awful.' Dragonfoot spoke without thinking and immediately regretted it as the elder spun around to face him again.

'How *awful*?!" He shouted. 'The dragons vanishing is awful, the fear of bandits is awful, not dreaming, stupid child, is not awful at all.' With that the elder stormed off, leaving Dragonfoot speechless in the shade of the tree.

Chapter 3

'I am Maximus'

'He's the grumpiest of the lot of them. I've no idea why they sent him to teach you about The Beforan — he has no clue about The Beforan and no patience.' A small voice spoke from inside the tree. 'And just for your information dreaming is a sore point — especially for him.'

This information intrigued Dragonfoot almost as much as the bodyless voice.

'Hmmm, interested now, are you? Like a bit of gossip, eh?' the voice continued in a playful way. 'Jealous, that's what he is. He once sought out one of those Dreamsellers, he did, desperate to dream he was. Gave them all his precious stones for one dream and after all that he didn't like it. Since then, he's been the grumpiest of the lot of the elders!'

'Oh' As this information sunk in, Dragonfoot looked up to see a small creature descend from one of the leaves.

'I am Maximus the tree nymph,' the tiny creature said while reaching out his hand to shake Dragonfoot's.

Dragonfoot smiled and placed his little finger into Maximus' hand and shook it, 'Very nice to meet you Maximus, I am...' and before he could finish Maximus said 'Dragonfoot. You are Dragonfoot, I know pretty much everything. It's handy being this little sometimes.'

'Everything?' Dragonfoot asked, 'could you teach me about the Beforan?'

'I most certainly could, and I most certainly will!' Maximus spoke with a smile as he jumped onto Dragonfoot's shoulder barely making a sound. 'Right so you, do you mind if we walk and talk? I need to get to the other side of the valley, and it'd take forever on my little legs. Don't worry – for you it'd be a quick stroll.' Maximus spoke quickly and decidedly. Dragonfoot began to walk. 'The other way!' Maximus shouted and pointed behind them, so Dragonfoot turned and began again.

'Well, what do you wanna know?' Maximus bluntly asked.

'Well, everything really,' Dragonfoot continued 'What is the Beforan?' He then paused reassessing what he actually wanted to know and then began again 'Why are the dragons vanishing? What are bandits? And why do Dragonfeet not dream?'

'Okay, okay, right so, may I make a suggestion?' Maximus advised, Dragonfoot nodded. 'You are asking all the wrong questions. Yes I can tell you the dragons are vanishing because the world is getting too small for their type of magic and until they learn to adapt they will not be welcome AND I could tell you about bandits,' (with that he spat on the ground then continued), 'h- orrible things are bandits – out to steal every bit of magic for themselves or to sell on and make themselves rich – they long to get their hands on a dragons egg as each one of its scales holds an unbelievable amount of magic and therefore they would become the richest things in all the universes! Old grumps back there is very paranoid as the tribe are currently protecting the last known dragon's egg and he's worried the bandits will be able to get through the magic barrier of Draig.'

With that he took a deep breath, 'but let me start by saying to you The Beforan is not long lost, it's vanished. The Dragonfeet Tribe can be so dramatic, especially when they can't fully explain things. But I know it is still about – but because they can't see it in their eyes it means it's *loong* lost.' The last bit he mimicked in the elders' old shaky voices.

Dragonfoot raised an eyebrow, he wasn't sure if vanished was any better than long lost but he supposed that would explain why he was young and alive. After a brief silence Dragonfoot quizzed Maximus. 'What are the right questions I should be asking then?'

'Now that is a good question' the little tree nymph said emphasizing his words by raising his index finger up in the air. 'Maybe ask who you are and how you got here? Also, it's worth asking where that little moth and plant vanished to yesterday while you're at it!'

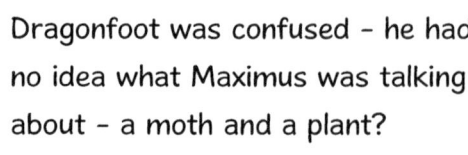

Dragonfoot was confused – he had no idea what Maximus was talking about – a moth and a plant?

Maximus knew very well he didn't, but he just loved to confuse people in order to show just how knowledgeable he was. 'Well don't you worry about my little moth friend, she's safe in Jadoo with Moon Grá chasing the moon.' He grinned broadly.

'Erm that's good I suppose... but how do you know?'

'I can't tell you all my secrets!' Maximus teased while crossing his arms and turning slightly away from Dragonfoot's face, then, swinging back round almost immediately with an even bigger smile on his face. 'Oh, alright I will tell you, what's a few secrets between friends eh!'

He rummaged in his tiny pocket and pulled out and even tinier pebble, with a hole right through it. He held it up proudly, 'This is my fallen stone – I found it on one of my many explorations. It's magical, as are most things in this world. If I look through the hole, I can see many a magical world.' He looked through it, demonstrating. 'Even *looong* lost ones!' he added with a wink.

Excitedly Dragonfoot hopped on the spot 'Can I see too?'

The tree nymph quickly popped the fallen stone back in his pocket.

'No. It found me so only I can use its magic. Maybe one day one will find you.'

Dragonfoot continued strolling on trying to hide his disappointment.

'How did I get here?' He asked after a long silence.

'I thought you'd never ask!' Maximus grabbed hold of Dragonfoot's ear and called inside 'you are a time traveller of sorts, a universe hopper, a magic leaper, a traveller of worlds!' He stretched out his arms as he spoke. He went on 'The greatest thing is, you can also transport other creatures and things to places — you are truly unique. You are YOU!' With that he flopped down on his bottom worn out by his own enthusiasm.

Dragonfoot looked to his shoulder where the tree nymph was getting back his breath, almost a little too nervous to ask the next question. 'How did I get here, to Draig?'

Maximus looked at Dragonfoot dumbfoundedly 'I *told* you... because you are a magic world time travelling universe hopper!!' Dragonfoot stared at the tree nymph, so Maximus continued in a slower tone bordering on condescending 'you magicked yourself and that blue-thorned bramble bush to Draig.'

'But why?'

Maximus had begun to get tired of Dragonfoot, 'Oh I don't know - maybe you were in danger or something? Anyway, this is my stop I'm off, thanks and all for the lift!' With that he hopped off of Dragonfoot's shoulder faster than Dragonfoot could say goodbye and scuttled off into the bushes ahead.

Poor Dragonfoot was now alone with even more questions than before only now he also had a fear of bandits and was worried he may magically go to another world at any point without meaning to. He sighed a big sigh then headed back towards Draig Valley; his shoulders heavy.

Chapter 4

The Bookworm and the Gift

Dragonfoot kicked his feet along the ground as he walked back to the valley, trying to make sense of the morning he had had when suddenly he saw a beautifully smooth stone with three clear holes directly through it. It reminded him of Maximus' fallen stone and without a second thought he whisked it up and placed it safely in his bag belt — he couldn't wait to show Bea his finding! Walking a little faster he pondered, maybe Bea had a fallen stone too, or if not, maybe they could share. Oh wait, Maximus had said only the finder can use it. He also remembered Maximus say his fallen stone had found him and for some reason this gave Dragonfoot a happy tingle in his tummy – he did a little hop and a skip as he neared Draig Valley.

When he arrived back Bea was looking perplexed and stamping the ground in random spots.

'What are you doing?' Dragonfoot asked.

Bea didn't even look up, just continued stamping the ground as she answered him 'I need to find the Bookworm. Where is he?' she grumped as she did one final big stamp on the dry ground. Her ears then began to twitch and a broad smile appeared on her face. 'Here he comes' she chuckled and sat down looking at the ground in front of her.

Dragonfoot had never heard of a Bookworm before and wasn't sure what to expect to see appearing from the ground. He sat gently next to Bea and waited, glancing at his friend and then to the ground. Within a few minutes the soil began to crumble away and a small, long creature appeared.

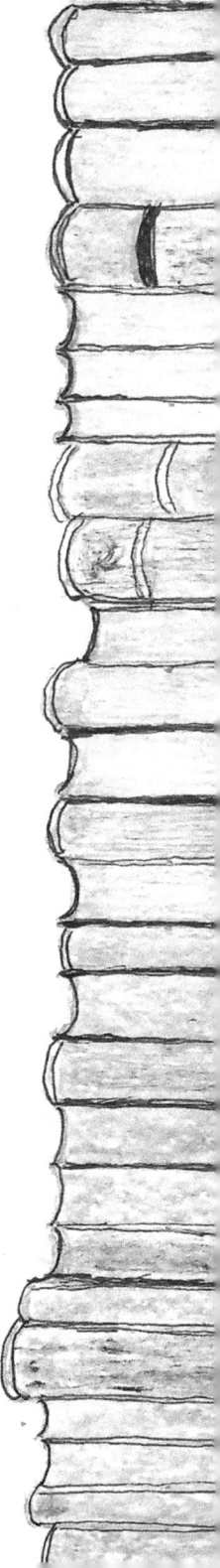

'Finally!' Bea groaned 'I've been trying to find you all morning!'

'Well, I've been busy,' the creature snapped back at Bea 'You wouldn't believe how many creatures have been looking for books lately.' The creature suddenly noticed Dragonfoot leaning towards him to get a closer look.

'Ahh so you're the new creature I have heard lots of rumbles about... hmmm... I have a book for you!' The creature then shot back down into the ground, Dragonfoot looked over at Bea who was looking rather smug.

'I knew he would have a book for you,' she whispered.

Dragonfoot smiled nervously, he wasn't really sure how well he could read in Draig tongue. He was scared maybe he couldn't read in any tongue! He gulped louder than he meant as the Bookworm reappeared from the dirt with a tiny little red book on its head.

'There' the Bookworm said as he threw the book in front of Dragonfoot. 'Oh, err, thank you,' Dragonfoot stuttered as he went to pick it up.

'Not yet!' the Bookworm snapped, startling Dragonfoot. The creature began to shiver, raising his nose up high in the air. Dragonfoot leant away from the Bookworm fearful of what was happening. The Bookworm stopped shivering and began to wiggle his nose and then lurching over suddenly let out a ginormous sneeze — snot and all — landing on and covering the tiny red book.

'Nearly ready now,' the Bookworm said. As the last word left the Bookworm's mouth the book began to sparkle and grow bigger and bigger. 'There, now it's the perfect size for you,' he proudly said and gestured for Dragonfoot to pick it up.

Reluctantly, Dragonfoot reached out and was pleasantly surprised and relieved that the book was nice and dry. Trying to look sensible, he examined the book cover. It really was a beautiful shade of red. He opened it slowly, deciding that he would pretend to be able to read whatever was inside whether he could or could not. To his absolute relief the pages were blank. He smiled and flicked through it — absolutely blank!

Bea looked confused — 'there's nothing in that book, Bookworm, what are you playing at?'

The Bookworm stretched up and looked at the white pages from over Dragonfoot's shoulder.

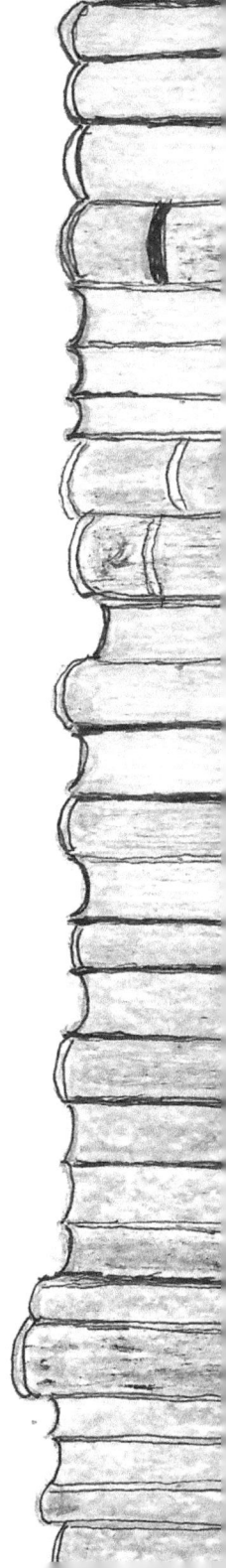

'Hmmm,' he began, 'how curious, how curious indeed. You appear to have received this book too early.' He chuckled, 'It doesn't look like it's been written yet.'

'Maybe it's a notebook,' Bea suggested.

The Bookworm spluttered in disgust at this. 'Absolutely not — do not attempt to write in that book!!'

'Ok then should he give it back to you until it *has* been written? There's no point whatsoever for him to have a blank book.'

The Bookworm started to retreat to his hole shaking his head.

'No he cannot give it back, I shan't take it, he can keep it and one day the words will appear — mark my words - it'll be the best book he's ever read! Now good day!' And with a flash he was gone.

Bea jumped angrily trying to catch him, but he was too quick. 'Sorry,' she said as she turned to Dragonfoot. 'I thought he'd give you a proper book, I thought it may cheer you up after having the morning with the grumpy Elder.' Dragonfoot appreciated the thought and placed the blank book in a pocket. Bea smiled - she was pleased to see him using her gift.

Chapter 5

A Bluff with a View

Days turned to weeks, weeks to months and soon the season was changing. Dragonfoot would keep checking his book gifted to him from the Bookworm but alas the pages still remained blank, though as he believed one day they would be full of words he took it upon himself to learn the different languages known around him. Draig tongue was tricky, but he found brownie and nymph easier and was soon fluent in those languages.

He was also, of course, still learning from Bea. By Autumn she had taught Dragonfoot so much about magic and the way of the Dragonfeet Tribe he really felt like he was becoming one of them - though the

elders reminded him whenever they could that he was *not* and only knew how to do magic *tricks* not true magic. Bea would tell him not to pay attention to their old ways, but it still would hurt. On these days he would go walking by himself practising languages and magic and embracing the beauty of the land around him - this always made him feel better.

One day, after the grumpiest of elders sneered at Dragonfoot as he tried to make a grey stone into a shiny red ruby only to make it disappear completely, Dragonfoot found himself walking further than he'd ever gone before. The scornful sneer had just about vanished from his mind when he found himself at the bottom of the largest bluff he'd ever seen! Without a second thought he climbed to the very highest point embracing the wonderful views. He could see forests, valleys, rivers, lakes, fields and then, in the far-off distance, he could have sworn he saw something in the sky - no not something, some things.

At first glance they looked like clouds, then, rubbing his eyes they appeared more like mountains floating in the sky. The mountains were all a different colour; red, blue, pink and green. Dragonfoot had never seen anything like these before and he rubbed his eyes again in disbelief, then they were gone. He turned one way then another trying to locate them again with no luck and then his

ears twitched. A strange noise, that seemed to be
coming from the valley, could be heard carried on the
warm breeze, but how could he hear something all
the way from Draig Valley up here? He looked across
in the direction of Draig and concentrated his ears
twitching fast.

'Help!' he heard, faint but clear. 'Help!'– again. Without
hesitation Dragonfoot began running, sliding and
jumping down the bank. He ran as fast as he could
back to Draig Valley.

Chapter 6

Jadoo

As he got closer to the valley Dragonfoot could hear screams and looking ahead he saw the valley in absolute chaos. Creatures were running everywhere grabbing their belongings, pushing each other out of the way. Dragonfoot began to sprint — he needed to find Bea - make sure she was ok. He seemed to be running for ages before he finally found himself in the middle of the mayhem.

Bandits! He was sure of it — they were tearing into the houses and shops — searching for something.

The dragons' egg! Dragonfoot slipped past the horrible creatures and made his way to the cave of the elders. The dragon was no longer there, her egg left in the middle of the room, unprotected. Without a second thought Dragonfoot ran to the egg and scooped it up, it was heavier than he had expected but thankfully his grasp was strong. He placed it as best he could on his back, securing it with materials he had in his belt bag. As he did so he could hear voices both from the entrance and further into the cave. He was sure the entrance was being blocked by bandits — they must be able to sense the egg was here.

Dragonfoot took a chance and made his way further into the cave hoping the other voices were of the Dragonfeet Tribe. Thankfully he was right, he was pleased to see their faces - even those of the grumpy elders.

Bea ran to him and hugged him, as she did, she noticed what was on his back.

'Dragonfoot, no, you mustn't take that,' the fear in her voice drained the colour from Dragonfoot's face.

'But I couldn't leave it - not to the bandits.' His voice was shaking. The shrill screams of the bandits were getting closer and louder.

'WE FLY NOW!' boomed the elders and with that the back of the cave opened to reveal blue skies. The Dragonfeet Tribe all started to stamp their feet, the noise almost unbearable. Dragonfoot began to stamp his too but Bea grabbed his arm.

'Don't,' she said 'just grab onto me as tight as you can when it's time. I mean it Dragonfoot - don't let go'.

'But where are we going?' Dragonfoot stuttered, Bea glanced around checking no one was listening before leaning in and whispering, 'the floating blue mountains.' The noise in the cave was so great Dragonfoot could barely make out the words but there was no time to ask again.

Sparks flew from the thundering clawed feet. Each member of the tribe began to grow in size and each grew wings - they began to spread out and fly into the sky. Dragonfoot did what Bea had said and before he knew it, they were soaring high into the clear sky. He clung on for dear life, his eyes shut tightly, scared of what he may see. His ears twitched as he could hear siren-like noises whizz past them. He opened his eyes and saw balls of flame flying through the air, some hitting tribe members, knocking them out of the sky. He closed his eyes again; his feet began to twitch. He wished he was anywhere else but here. He hugged Bea closer as he wished for their safety. Sparks began to fly from his foot...

Dragonfoot's grip was tight yet suddenly his arms fell towards each other, he opened his eyes, his arms frantically grappling for Bea, but she was not there. He began to fall through the sky, faster and faster. He balled up waiting for the impact, but no impact came. To his shock, and relief, he gently landed on a grassy hillside. He sat up, staring at the sky, searching for the tribe in flight – willing them to appear, safe. The sky though seemed different, it was now pink, not blue, and was speckled with wispy white clouds.

Dragonfoot suddenly reached to his back to make sure the egg was still there. He sighed with relief when he felt its scaled shell. Still sat on the grass he hugged his knees to his chest for comfort, glancing down at his feet as he did so, and there on the ankle of his small foot was another marking.

He jumped up – he'd done it again! But how? Dragonfoot now on his feet darted his head around trying to figure out where he was and how he could get back. Suddenly a voice came from out of nowhere.

'Oh no, no, no, that won't do at all, no, no, not here, not in Jadoo.'

Startled, Dragonfoot turned around to see where the voice had come from and there behind him was a hunched-over woman with a face that looked like the bark of a tree - knots and all.

Dragonfoot let out a little scream and stumbled back, not his finest moment, and the woman looked up at him with disgust.

'What's wrong child... creature... thing,' she spoke as she studied him.

'I'm Dragonfoot' he said as he studied her back.

'Well, whatever you are - have you never seen a tree keeper before? I look fairly good for my age, but you, you creature Dragonfoot, you will not do at all! Not like that!'

Dragonfoot tried to hide his foot thinking it was that she was referring to but as he did the tree keeper spat, 'Not that you fool! That!' and pointed at the Dragons egg on his back. 'You can't have that on full display – not here - especially not so close to you know who and you know whats!'

Dragonfoot hadn't the slightest idea what this hag was talking about as he watched her grabbing large leaves and shoving them in his hands.

'Quick! Hide that egg, oh you must do it now! Before my sister arrives back or she'll grind it up and drink it as tea!!!'

Horrified, Dragonfoot did as the tree keeper instructed. It took him a few attempts and hits on the head from her before she was satisfied the egg was hidden proficiently in a bag made of leaves but once she was, her face softened, slightly. It felt to Dragonfoot like she was trying to smile - he was pleased as his head was getting quite sore.

'There, that's better' she said, positively grinning now, 'would like some tea?'

Dragonfoot hesitated, a little worried what type of 'tea' she was meaning. The Tree Keeper saw this and with a kind of part cough part chuckle she elaborated, 'Mint tea, I grow the mint myself in my garden. I'm not into all that kind of magic that involves crushing up live things and consuming them. Always seemed a bit icky to me.' With a sigh of relief Dragonfoot accepted her offer of mint tea and followed as she hobbled back to a large hollow tree trunk, which was her home. It was warm and cozy and the tea was sweet and refreshing.

'Now where are you going with that thing?' the Tree Keeper asked with concern. Dragonfoot breathed deeply. 'I'm not sure,' he admitted 'I need to get it somewhere safe, but where that is I have no idea.' He looked down and fiddled with the handle of his cup. The Tree Keeper placed her gnarly hand gently on his, 'When you are near, the blue moon will guide you,' she topped up their tea. 'A, *you know what*, is a very magical thing. There is a place on the other side of Jadoo where magical objects can be safe. Do you think you can get it there?'

Dragonfoot thought briefly, 'and it would be completely safe there – not sold, or eaten or destroyed?' She nodded her head, 'completely safe' she confirmed. 'Then I can, and I will,' Dragonfoot said and he stood up. As he did so, a shrieking came from outside making them both jump. Flustered, the Tree Keeper jumped to her feet.

'My sister, she's back, quickly,' she began shoving items into Dragonfoot's hands. A *ginormous* eye peered into the hollow, the pupil slit like that of a snake.

'Sister, what are you doing? I smell something new – are you playing with potions again?' A harsh, sharp voice, pierced through the warmth of the room.

'Oh shoo,' the Tree Keeper said, 'can't you see I have a customer; he's looking to get his clothes repaired, look at them tears and rips all over the place.' She spoke not looking towards her sister but instead fussing around Dragonfoot, placing new shorts and top on him. 'There that's better,' she said stepping back admiring her work, Dragonfoot stayed silent - frozen to the spot with fear. The eye lingered a while, then, thankfully vanished with the same shriek as it had appeared.

The Tree Keeper and Dragonfoot stood in silence for a few moments. Finally, the Tree Keeper gave a long sigh of relief and immediately started to push Dragonfoot out.

'You must go now,' she said, the panic in her voice worried Dragonfoot.

'What about these clothes you've put on me?'

'Keep them, be it a gift to welcome you to Jadoo!' she said as she rushed him out and towards a path. 'Follow this path and you'll come to a market - vanish in the crowds — my sister hates crowds -she'd never follow you there. And please, please, please keep that thing hidden at ALL times!'

Dragonfoot had to jog a little as the Tree Keeper pushed him with all her might, he turned to bid her farewell, but she was gone. Alone again — ah - not alone - he still had the Dragon egg with him. He could feel it's warmth against his back and it gave some comfort as he began down the path towards the market the Tree Keeper spoke of.

Chapter 7

The Storyteller

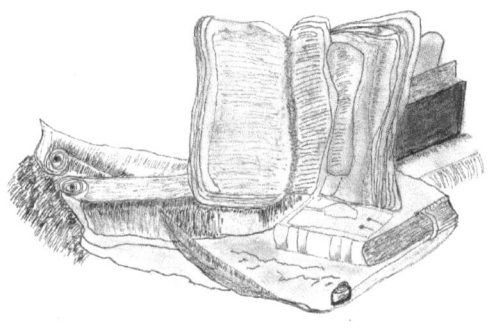

Dragonfoot reached the bustling little market. He looked around in awe. A flutter of excitement filled his tummy as his eyes took everything in. There were stalls for as far as the eye could see - fairies selling flowers; elves selling toys; centaurs selling boots. Dragonfoot had to see them all!

The first stall he came to was made up of an array of beautiful flowers - all the colours you could imagine - two fairies were delicately painting each petal. They glanced up at

Dragonfoot, he smiled and raised his hand, he had the urge to touch one of the flowers, they looked so soft. Quickly one of the fairies batted his hand away.

'No! no! no! You do not touch until you buy – now shoo!' It said waving its arms at Dragonfoot, wings fluttering manically. Dragonfoot put his hand straight back in his pocket, lowered his head and strolled on.

The next stall was just as bright and colourful as the one before. A lady and two young girls sat behind the stall, each wearing a single stone necklace. The girls were singing a song he recognized - a song about witches of the earth and sky – the song Bea used to sing. He stopped, and as he listened, he began to watch the lady behind the stall who seemed to be painting, though Dragonfoot could see no paint pots or brushes. He watched closely as she moved her fingertips across the page barely touching the linen canvas yet colours and images so clear appeared beneath her dancing fingers.

Lost in the moment, the sounds around him faded - he could have sworn the picture she was painting was moving as he watched. The image was of swirling clouds reflecting the colours of a sunset over fields of purple heathers. Dragonfoot felt a warm glow as he saw the heathers, he remembered how free he felt as he had run in them in Draig.

Suddenly the noises of the bustling marketplace returned to him and they seemed louder. Dragonfoot glanced around looking to see what the noise was about and then he clocked a crowd at the end of the street. They gasped and laughed at whatever it was that was in front of them – Dragonfoot had to have a closer look! He repositioned the Dragon egg and tightened it onto his back, then walked slowly towards the animated crowd. He was so focused on the crowd he hadn't realised there was a creature watching him - and the egg - as he passed. This creature, with beady eyes, stared intently at him, and slowly began to follow him as he made his way through the crowd.

The lady who had been painting, saw the creature in pursuit of Dragonfoot. She knew who he was and knew he was bad news. Quickly she called her daughters to be ready.

As Dragonfoot made his way through the crowd he saw a man sat cross-legged on the ground wearing a long black hooded cloak. His head was facing the sky, his mouth spinning a tale so wonderful and exciting the crowd was entranced. Every so often Dragonfoot caught a glimpse of the man's tongue - it was covered in words, changing constantly as he spoke. From his eyes shone lights creating a floating orb in which his story came to life. Dragonfoot, along with the majority of the crowd, was mesmerized. As the man's story came to an end the orb and lights faded, he straightened his head and blinked a few times as though awakening from a dream - the words from his tongue vanished.

Dragonfoot stepped towards the man who was now counting the money people had thrown. Either side of him lay a large dog curled up, sleeping soundly. Dragonfoot was now directly in front of him and the man, seeing one large, clawed foot, looked up. When his eyes met Dragonfoot's he offered a broad smile.

'Hello and welcome.' He spoke with a velvety voice. Putting out his hand, his cloak slipped up his arm revealing brightly coloured tattoos - as was his whole body it seemed. The painted man looked directly into Dragonfoot's eyes, and they were like none Dragonfoot had ever seen before — not blue or brown but many, many colours. Instead of solid black irises the man's were made up of hundreds of tiny words, constantly moving and changing - just like the ones that had been on his tongue as he'd weaved his tale. Dragonfoot blinked and rubbed his eyes.

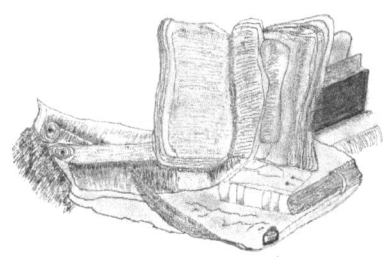

'I'm the Storyteller,' the man said, still smiling broadly.

Dragonfoot stalled for a second — Bea had told him about Storytellers - they're not be trusted, she'd said -

they rob you blind, you must never believe a word they say — yet this man, this Storyteller seemed genuine. Dragonfoot held out his hand and shook the Storyteller's hand.

'I'm Dragonfoot,' he said.

'Ah, I have heard whispers about a new creature in Jadoo' the Storyteller said, grinning. Suddenly his grin was gone and his eyes started to dart around the crowd.

Dragonfoot heard a rustling and then as he turned, he saw something leaping out of the crowd - reaching out its spindly arms - trying to grab his leaf bag which held the Dragon's egg. He stumbled back in shock. Then a scream - that rivalled that of a banshee - rang out through the marketplace.

Stallholders and customers ran around as the lady and her daughters walked towards the creature. The stones on their necklaces shone as thunder began to clash overhead. The smallest daughter screamed again, the thing cowered, covering its ears in pain - the eldest daughter raised her hand, and a mighty gust of wind swept the creature off its feet. The lady raised both arms to the sky, hail thundered down and mighty bolts of lightning started to strike the ground around the creature.

The Storyteller reached his hand out and grabbed Dragonfoot.

'Quick! Follow me! The witches will deal with that bandit!' His dogs ran ahead of them guiding them through the maze of colour, noise, confusion and stallholders running and flying around in panic.

They didn't have to run too far before the skies were clear and blue again, the sun shining brightly. Out of breath they slowed to a walk. Dragonfoot looked back towards the market, a large dark grey cloud enveloped the area.

Soon they had arrived at a tiny hole in the ground. The Storyteller stomped his foot twice and the hole increased, allowing the four of them to climb down, then closed quickly behind them.

'Home,' the Storyteller sighed with relief. Once the candles were lit, Dragonfoot could see around this burrow — there were pages and pages of stories and drawings everywhere.

'What just happened?' Dragonfoot asked trying to calm his thoughts.

'A bandit,' the Storyteller spat out the words looking worried. 'I thought they were all trapped, especially when I saw that on your back' he said scratching the back of his neck. 'They're nasty things, always out to steal and my friend you have the most valuable thing - the thing they've been searching for years for.' He rubbed his forehead and paced.

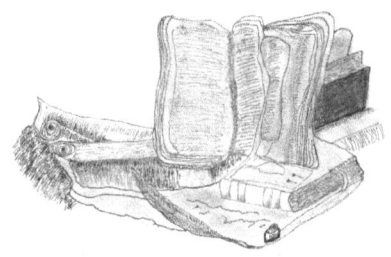

Dragonfoot glanced to his back to check on the egg, and there he saw one tiny scale on show.

'Oh.' He suddenly felt a wave of guilt as he remembered what the Tree Keeper had specifically told him to do 'I thought it was still hidden'. Covering the scale up he turned to the Storyteller.

'Where did you think the bandits were trapped?'

With this question all the colour drained from the Storyteller's face and a sinking feeling came over Dragonfoot as he remembered, only the day before, the devastation the bandits were causing in Draig Valley. The Storyteller looked down and barely croaked the word 'Draig.'

'But how did they get there?' Dragonfoot was so confused and then, seeing the guilt on the Storyteller's face, he began to piece it together.

'But how?' Dragonfoot started to feel the anger bubbling up inside of him.

Without saying a word, the Storyteller pulled up his sleeve revealing similar marks to those on Dragonfoot's leg.

'You' Dragonfoot stuttered pointing at the Draig symbol. 'But why?'

The Storyteller let his sleeve fall covering the symbols once more.

'Dragonfoot, trust me, I didn't think they'd be able to do as much damage as they appear to have done.' He rubbed his neck again nervously. 'They got me to help them get to Draig, but I thought I was leading them into a trap – I thought the Dragonfeet Tribe would be able to overcome them easily.'

Dragonfoot was getting angrier and stamped his foot.

'Well, they weren't able to - Draig is completely destroyed' he tensed his fists.

The Storyteller continued trying to explain. 'But the tribe, I heard, got away, didn't they? And you, you saved the egg.' He sighed. 'I thought I had transported *all* the bandits - there is no way they can get back to Jadoo - not without the egg. I was so relieved when I heard the whispers of the strange creature appearing here in Jadoo - but then - just there - in the market, I realized I'd failed — there are still some here.' His eyes welled up, 'I'm so sorry.'

Dragonfoot could barely bring himself to look at the Storyteller. Everything Bea had said was true. He secured the leaf bag on his back making sure the Dragon's egg was hidden completely, adjusted his belt bag and began to look for a way out.

'Where are you going?' the Storyteller asked. 'Please, trust me, you are safe here.'

'Show me the way out, now,' Dragonfoot continued to look for an exit, still clearly angry.

 The Storyteller, knowing there was nothing he could say to make Dragonfoot stay, directed him to the corner of the burrow and reached into his cloak.

'Here, Dragonfoot,' he held out a silver object, 'I now know what I did was wrong. I cannot keep you here, but please take this with you it may help.'

Dragonfoot looked down at the object. It appeared to be a silver tongue. He was very hesitant to touch it let alone take it with him. Sensing Dragonfoot's reluctance, the Storyteller explained.

'This is my father's silver tongue. He was known to be able to get out of any situation thanks to this. Take it and it will help you if you ever need it.'

Dragonfoot couldn't help but look a little disgusted. 'I have to put it in my mouth?' he asked. The Storyteller returned his disgusted look.

'No, ugh gosh no, that is gross. No, no holding it should be sufficient.'

Dragonfoot, relieved by this answer and believing the Storyteller was genuinely sorry, took the silver tongue and placed it in one of the pockets of the belt bag. The Storyteller stomped his foot once and a hole to the outside world opened above them.

'Head north, Dragonfoot, the paths are safer that way' the Storyteller advised and with that Dragonfoot climbed quickly out, but before he left, he looked back at the Storyteller.

'Thank you' he said.

With a nod the Storyteller's burrow closed once more and Dragonfoot began on his journey north.

Chapter 8

The Dreamseller

It appeared the Storyteller had been right - the path heading north seemed safe and thankfully was also lined with berry bushes. Dragonfoot tucked into the beautiful fruit as he walked along, still unsure as to where he was heading.

As he walked and the night drew in, the world around him became shrouded in darkness. The moon was but a sliver - it's glow barely reaching the path before him. Dragonfoot took a deep breath in - he hated to admit it but he felt scared of the dark. However, determined to continue, he kept walking on.

A little further down the path he saw a tall figure wearing a beautiful cloak that sparkled with a map of the constellations and a hood covering all but its mouth.

As Dragonfoot approached this stranger he understood exactly who it was and knew he need not be scared.

It was a Dreamseller. Dragonfoot had heard of them many times but had never seen one before. It was said they appeared when a special dream was being sought.

'May we walk with you.' A silky voice spoke showing glimpses of bright white star-like teeth. Relieved to have some company, Dragonfoot agreed quickly and the two of them continued down the dark path.

As they walked Dragonfoot couldn't help but wonder why they had appeared to him. He wasn't seeking a dream and definitely had no means to buy a dream from them, though feared bringing this up in case they left again.

The Dreamseller smiled. 'You don't seek a dream.' Dragonfoot shook his head. 'Then why do you feel we are here?' they continued earnestly.

Dragonfoot thought for a while and then hesitatingly said 'I think maybe you appeared to me because I was,' he paused, almost embarrassed to continue, 'scared of the dark.' The Dreamseller chuckled and they nodded their head.

'Yes, I think you may be right' they smiled 'but the dark should not worry you, though the world around you may look differently I can assure you it is the same as if it were broad daylight. I find the darkness calming.' With that, they took a deep breath in through their nose and gently released it out from their mouths. Dragonfoot copied them and felt the calmness come over him. He smiled and looked ahead, yes it was very dark, but now he was sure the trees ahead were just trees and not the scary giants he had imagined before. He smiled again, and that thing rolling towards them - that was just a rock and not a goblin about to knock them down... but the rock was getting closer, and he could see it definitely was a goblin and most definitely getting closer very quickly.

Dragonfoot jumped to one side as the rolling goblin sped past them followed by several more. The Dreamseller didn't even flinch as they narrowly missed them. They turned to Dragonfoot and gestured for him to step back onto the path.

'Don't worry Dragonfoot, it's just a family of goblins, they always travel at night as it's much cooler for them and less busy — they really do not like crowds big or small. Come to think of it, I don't think most creatures like goblins either, though they really are harmless - just a bit grumpy and a little smelly.'

Dragonfoot had to do a little hop and a skip to catch up with the Dreamseller, keeping his eyes peeled for any more rolling creatures of the night. The two companions walked and talked until smiling their large smile the Dreamseller pointed to the east.

'The sun will be rising soon; we will need to be gone. But before we do, we have something for you.'

Dragonfoot looked up at the figure as they lifted their cloak revealing eyes the colour of midnight. Whole universes seemed to swirl in their depths. Dragonfoot watched mesmerised as the Dreamseller hummed a soothing tune. The sun began to rise. The Dreamseller placed their cloak over their eyes once more and smiled. Placing something in Dragonfoot's hand and gently closing it to a fist they said, 'This dream is for you to use when you really need it.' They spoke almost in a whisper now, 'Always remember Dragonfoot there's no more magical place in this world than that of our dreams' and with that they faded into the light of the dawn.

Slowly opening his fist, Dragonfoot saw he was holding a beautiful shimmering moonstone. After giving it a happy squeeze he placed it safely in a pocket and started again along the path. He didn't get too much further before he yawned a big yawn – he'd almost forgotten he had not rested for nearly two days now! Finding a small cluster of bushes, he climbed in, hiding himself and the Dragon egg and curled up to rest. He figured an hour's sleep would do him wonders and he'd then be on his way.

The sun rose and set three times before Dragonfoot finally woke. With a big stretch he emerged from his bush cocoon. There was a noticeable chill in the air and with a shudder Dragonfoot tightened his clothing and bag before continuing north, though he could have sworn the path had changed somehow. Shrugging off his thought he began with a hop and a skip. Before too long he saw a small object on the path ahead, as he came closer, he saw it was a small golden key. He looked around. He picked it up wondering how it could have gotten here - knowing someone must be missing it - but he had not seen any creatures on this path, so thought maybe they were ahead. Placing it safely in a pocket he continued on. He did not notice that from the undergrowth a pair of black beady eyes were watching him - the same beady eyes he had encountered from the marketplace.

The black-eyed creature hid well as he began to track Dragonfoot, never letting him out of his sight. Oh, how he wanted to swoop in and grab the dragon's egg, but he knew this time he'd have to wait - he could not handle another embarrassment. Patiently he waited, for days watching Dragonfoot at a distance, willing him to get to the crossroads quickly for that was where he would have the upper hand. You see, he had sent his finder fleas ahead of him to send word to the other bandits that were still in Jadoo to meet him at the crossroads.

Finder fleas are amazing little creatures, quick, intelligent and agile, they can cover vast distances in no time without being seen – perfect for sending secret messages.

Chapter 9

The Crossroads

Dragonfoot hobbled now as the path below his feet became harder and harder. He held the egg closer; it had become a comfort to him, this egg meant he was not alone. The days had started to turn to night much faster now and this night was no different; he now found himself at a standstill. The moon was almost full so he could clearly see the split in the path ahead, but he didn't know which way he should go and he was getting tired. He slumped to the ground and cuddled the egg. The egg felt warm, and he could sense the growing dragon move within its shell. 'I'll get us there safely' Dragonfoot thought out loud.

'Where?' said a voice suddenly

'Yes, where?' another piped up, and a third continued, in a rather spiteful manner, 'How are you going to do that when you can't even decide which path is best?'.

Dragonfoot jumped to his feet and looked all around but he could not see where these voices had come from.

'He can hear us' said the first.

'But the real test is if he can *see* us,' the second continued.

Dragonfoot's eyes darted around but there was nothing but darkness. His clawed foot began to twitch on the ground, this was something it would do if he felt scared. Faster it twitched then a spark of light flew up making the owners of the voices clear as day. An unusual creature - or creatures - he was unsure, for it had one body but three very different heads.

'It's rude to stare,' one head said whilst the other two smiled broadly.

'I knew he'd be able to see us,' one said excitedly to the other while the third just rolled their eyes and tried to cross its arms — Dragonfoot saw this head only controlled the right arm and seemed frustrated when her other heads wouldn't comply and help her cross the left. She grunted as she thrust her right arm back down to her side.

'What are you?' Dragonfoot finally said as he stared at the creature and its rather beautiful heads.

'Do you not know of us?' one voice said, quickly followed by the other. 'We go by many names, but we are certainly not a *what* we are goddesses!' She spat the last part of the sentence in disgust at Dragonfoot's impolite comment. He felt himself blush red; he hadn't meant to insult them. He looked down, remembering the stories the elders of the Dragonfeet tribe would tell him of a creature of the crossroads. He glanced about again, of course he was at a crossroads – how did he not realise?

'I'm sorry,' he quietly said, 'I am weary from travelling and had not noticed where I was.'

One of the heads interrupted, 'and I suppose you haven't a gift for us? Huh!'

Dragonfoot, taken aback by the bluntness, blushing again, fumbled in his pockets. He slowly took out the fallen stone he'd found in Draig. –

'I have only this' he said lifting the stone towards the goddesses. They gave a collective gasp – 'Oh no, we mustn't take that from you. A fallen stone with three holes is such a rare find.'

'He doesn't even know what it is!' Scoffed one goddess.

'Then we must tell him. Why you have to be so cruel sister I will never know.' The kindly goddess looked to Dragonfoot and gestured for him to return the stone to his pocket. 'You see, a stone with a hole right through it is known by many different names throughout the many worlds we know of, but in all these worlds it is known especially for its magic properties. It not only brings luck to the finder but it also allows them to peer through to other worlds -be it the fairy realms or pixie woods -no world is forbidden to it. A stone with three holes, though is a rarity indeed.'

'Three is one of the most magical of numbers. Threefold luck, threefold magic' the third goddess jumped in excitedly. 'You can even ask it to show you what you seek. If you misplace something, ask the stone and it will show you!' She raised her hand to try to clap it with the other but the goddess in charge of the right hand held it still and just glared in disgust at the giddy display.

'I see no reason why you are so happy - I see no gift for us. Unless, of course, he has something in that big bag on his back that may be worthy.' With that she poked the bag. 'If not that then maybe *he* should be our gift, he'd look good stuffed and on my altar.' She spoke without blinking.

Dragonfoot became very nervous. He did not feel this was said as a bad joke from the goddess and knowing he had no gift for them in exchange for a safe crossing, became fearful for his life. Frantically he thought - He knew he couldn't give them a gift he had himself been given — that would have been rude -and the key was not his to give. He tugged the bag tighter onto his back, scared they may see the dragon's egg and take it for themselves. Then he remembered the Storyteller's gift. He held onto the silver tongue tightly.

'The gift I offer you in return for my safe pass is not one you may grasp in your hands - for that would not be fair for three goddesses as strong and wise as you are. No, my gift comes in the form of words — words that you may all keep in your minds as a memory forever. One you may call upon whenever you may choose' and with that Dragonfoot told the most beautiful story about the worlds he had been to and the wonders he had seen.

When his tale came to an end the Goddesses looked in wonder – even the grumpy one had now softened, almost warming to this strange creature before her.

'Fine, then we won't eat you,' she said turning her head slightly to hide the tiny tear appearing.

'You may pass,' the goddesses said in unison. Dragonfoot almost jumped for joy but then realised he wasn't sure where he should go. Should he carry on north — surely, he should need to turn at some point.

'Thank you, but I don't know where I should go,' he said but as he looked up the Goddesses were nowhere to be seen. There seemed to be a lot of vanishing in this world, Dragonfoot thought as he scratched his head.

He wasn't alone for long as suddenly; he found himself surrounded by four creepy looking creatures. Turning, he saw the bandit that had tried to get him at the marketplace. He gasped, stumbling backwards. The bandit behind him, a spindly skeleton-like creature with wild hair, pushed him hard on his back almost knocking him to the ground. Dragonfoot was so scared. He fell forward trying to keep his footing, but as he did the third and fourth bandits jumped on his back pulling at his bag trying to get hold of the dragon's egg. He tugged hard on the straps of the bag and hearing a ripping noise Dragonfoot's heart sank. The egg flew down on the ground shimmering in the moonlight. Dragonfoot was flung aside with such force it made him dizzy. He shook his head and looked towards the egg.

To his dismay all four bandits were on top of it, but luckily, they were too busy trying to tear each other off it so the egg remained unharmed - for now.

Dragonfoot felt his foot begin to twitch, sparks began to fly, he felt an overwhelming anger bubbling in his stomach and before he knew what was happening, he had launched himself directly at the four thieves in front of him. Bowling them over, he sent them flying in all different directions. Seizing his chance, he scooped up the egg and ran — sparks still flying wildly from his clawed foot. Unfortunately, the bandits recovered quickly and Dragonfoot didn't get far before the four had tackled him to the ground. Desperately he clung to the egg, closing his eyes in fear. Then suddenly their sharp grip on him loosened.

'Where's it gone?' hissed one of them.

'It must have rolled off in the scuffle, look over there, I'll look here' barked another angrily.

Dragonfoot slowly opened his eyes and looked into his empty arms. There were a few sparkles of magic left in his hands, and he knew what had happened. It hadn't rolled away — he had magicked it away — but where? His heart felt broken, but he didn't have time to allow his tears to come. If he stood any chance of finding the dragon's egg again, before these horrible creatures, he had first to get himself away from them and fast! Taking his opportunity, he curled up in a ball and rolled like he had seen the goblins doing, away from the arguing bandits, down a path unknown.

Chapter 10

Solas Grey

Dragonfoot rolled until dawn. Feeling dizzy and nauseous he lay on the ground watching the sun rise and trying to collect his thoughts. As he pondered, he felt his eyes begin to close. At first, he tried fighting it but then gave in, allowing his body to relax in the dewy grass. He fell into a deep yet short slumber where he dreamed so vividly about flying dragons, storytellers, weather witches, bandits and floating mountains – one of which stood out the most – a fantastic array of blues.

'Floating blue mountains!' Dragonfoot's eyes suddenly opened as he shouted these words - that's where Bea had said they were heading, he was sure.

Remembering what the Crossroads Goddess had told him about his fallen stone find he grabbed it from one of his pockets and held it up to his eye – nothing happened. He was staring through the hole and seeing the same grass where he was now sitting. Shaking the stone in his hand he tried again, frustrated – what was he doing wrong? Was he looking

through the wrong hole? He closed his eyes and took three deep breaths. Raising the stone to his eye he slowly opened them whispering 'show me the blue mountains'. This time the stone began to glow, the holes began to sparkle shades of gold, almost too bright and dazzling his eye a little, before he saw the beautiful floating mountains with the blue one in the centre. He saw them floating so smoothly in the sky – they were mesmerizing.

He could have watched the floating mountains forever, but Dragonfoot remembered the dragon egg and closing his eyes again he whispered, 'show me the dragon's egg.' As he opened them, he saw the beautiful shimmer of the scaled egg. Sighing with relief he started looking around the egg trying to figure out where it was. As he was doing this, he became distracted by a clatter of noise coming towards him. Quickly he instinctively slid the fallen stone safely back in its pocket just as a large wooden-wheeled cart appeared on the path beside his grassy bed.

The cart was being pulled by two amazing animals that Dragonfoot had never seen before. Such a sight! They looked to Dragonfoot like an animal jigsaw gone wrong but fascinating all the same. They had the head of a peacock, the body of a lion and the tail of a snake. They had three feet - one was an elephant's – thick and heavy; another was a deer's-slender and light; the third was a tiger's padded and muscular. Dragonfoot couldn't help but stare in wonderment. The driver of the cart saw Dragonfoot's interest and slowed down, happily showing off his *pets*.

'Beautiful, eh?'

The deep voice boomed, making Dragonfoot jump to his feet.

'Never seen anything like them before, eh?' the voice continued in a boastful manner. A head peered down from the cart, dark hair slicked back to a bun, and clothes so bright and colourful it rivalled the feathers of the most exotic parrot. He secured the reigns and then jumped down and, to Dragonfoot's surprise, the driver was fairly short of stature. This seemed to have also shocked the stranger himself as he gave a nervous cough then carried on, 'They're my pets, they're beautiful and very well trained, I have had them since they were but eggs themselves. Hybrids they are, do you know what that means?' Not waiting for a reply he continued, 'Basically, a hybrid is a thing made by combining different elements or creatures – usually only the best bits – that's the case with these two beauties anyway.'

He spoke with his chest puffed out and his hands on his hips. Looking Dragonfoot up and down, he continued, 'You seem to be a bit of a hybrid yourself'. At first, Dragonfoot didn't know what he meant and the stranger, seeing his odd look, pointed to his clawed foot. Dragonfoot began to blush. Hybrid was a word he had never heard used to describe himself before. 'Anyway,' the stranger said clapping his hands together, 'no time to chat really, I like to keep the sun on my back — I'm happy for you to join me if you'd like?'

Although they had just met, Dragonfoot felt a fondness to this stranger and happily accepted his offer. Not really knowing where he needed to go but liking the idea of company, Dragonfoot climbed onto the back of the cart as the stranger positioned himself with the reigns ready to get going. He gave a hearty chuckle.

'I just realised I've not introduced myself — the name is Solas Grey.' He turned to shake Dragonfoot's hand. Solas had a strong handshake.

'I'm Dragonfoot,'

He was quite pleased when Solas turned back to face his pets and with a quick couple of snaps at the reigns the animals began to gallop along the path.

The journey was bumpy, but Dragonfoot didn't mind, he was busy admiring Solas' brightly coloured coat. It had a large sun on the back - the main colour being yellow - but the rays of the sun were an array of many different colours — red, pink, blue and green.

'Where are you travelling to friend?' Solas called back as Dragonfoot was about to ask Solas about the picture on his coat.

'Ehm, I am mainly heading for the floating blue mountains, but I have to find something first, and I don't know where it is.'

Solas raised his eyebrow slightly.

'I will find it though' Dragonfoot said assuring himself as much as his new friend. Solas smiled nodding his head.

'My friend,' Solas began thoughtfully, 'may I offer you advice, for I have been on one of the floating mountains before, be it many moons ago — but I remember it as yesterday.' He smiled to the sky as he continued, 'The floating mountains are hard to find — they're forever moving you see — if you find them before you find the other thing you seek you cannot turn away — you must jump on. Please trust me on that one.'

Dragonfoot had never thought about how he would get onto a floating mountain if he were to find one — he hadn't realised they would move. He began to blush a little - partly because of embarrassment about how little he knew about this land and a little because of the fear he may not have the chance to find the Dragon's egg. His tummy began to have the same sinking feeling it had when he first realised, he had magicked the egg away.

Discretely, Dragonfoot got out the fallen stone and looked through it, once more wishing to see the Dragon's egg – each time the image came quicker and sharper. Straining his eyes he looked at the egg and its surroundings, searching for any clue as to where it may be. His ears began to twitch, and he realised he could hear where it was also and listening carefully, he could hear the faint flow of water. It was then that he

also noticed the Dragon's egg had a crack appearing. Dragonfoot was unsure if this meant it was hatching but if so, he needed to get to it quickly or else what would happen to the little dragon. A tear ran down his cheek as he put the fallen stone back in his pocket.

There was a sudden chill in the air, and then the rain began. Solas grumbled loudly.

'The Weather Witches are at it again,' he said shaking his head and steering the cart to shelter, 'I had been promised sunshine, hhmmph, do you call this sunshine?'

Dragonfoot wasn't sure if Solas wanted him to answer but before he could, Solas continued shouting to the sky 'DO YOU CALL THIS SUNSHINE??'

Dragonfoot was worried he'd gone mad but as he looked up too, he saw several witches flying overhead, cackling as they waved down to them.

'Serves me right I suppose,' Solas said jumping down from his cart and securing it to a nearby tree. 'I should never have tried to borrow a weather stone.' Then looking back up to the skies he shouted: 'BUT I DIDN'T MANAGE TO GET ONE, DID I?' Waving his arm in the air showing a nasty burn on his wrist. It then began to hail.

'Maybe it's best not to shout at them?' Dragonfoot spoke softly as he climbed down from the cart. 'It seems like you are making them more angry.' Solas covered his wrist back up.

'I only wanted to borrow the weather stone you know,' he looked down to the ground. 'My people needed the weather to improve for our crops, I didn't mean to anger them so.' Pausing to watch the hail stones hit the ground for a second. 'They really do keep a grudge.' Then giving a big shrug and stretch he said 'Anyway that's my travelling done for the day, I only travel when the sun is on my back, no sun, no travelling. Sorry Dragonfoot, now you are more than welcome to stay with me, but I know that look in your eye. I was a young man once, determined to finish my quests. But may I give you one more piece of advice. Take that path.'

The last bit he almost whispered as he pointed to an overgrown path. Winking at Dragonfoot, he patted him on his back.

Chapter 11

Moon Grá

The tree coverage sheltered Dragonfoot from the hail and rain though it also cast a darkness on the already creepy path ahead. Gulping loudly, he started to walk a little faster than before, with thoughts of the dragon's egg cracking spurring him on. The day quickly turned to night, the clouds drifted away, and the weather eased, making way for a large open sky. Dragonfoot could see the moon was full as he came to a clearing. He looked up in wonder, it was so magnificent. Suddenly he had stumbled over something, something that shouted loudly: 'Ooooowwww!'

'I'm so so sorry' Dragonfoot spluttered as he brushed himself off and looked back to see what he had tripped over. There was a huge cloud of moths surrounding something – they were all shapes and sizes and fluttering around madly. It was hard to make out what was beyond them.

Dragonfoot rubbed his eyes trying to see a little clearer and began to make out an unusual individual dusting herself down and shaking her head. Gently batting the moths aside, this 'being' stepped towards Dragonfoot and scowled. Her face was half-darkness and half-light - in fact this 'half and half' continued to the tips of her crazy nest of hair and to her delicate little toes. Strangely, it was not a straight line of dark and light. It was almost as if she had been splattered with a paint brush, so bits of darkness had gone on the light side and vice-versa. She was so beautiful — even when she was scowling.

Seeing her, Dragonfoot was lost for words. The creature's scowl dissipated and changed into the biggest smile he had ever seen.

'I know, I'm nearly as exquisite as the moon,' she chuckled as she flicked her hair dramatically. Dragonfoot blushed, this made her laugh out loud. 'I'm Moon Grá,' she said, 'and you are? Other than clumsy that is.'

Dragonfoot chuckled at this as he tried to find the words, 'I'm Dragonfoot,' he spoke gently.

'That explains the clumsiness,' Moon Grá joked. 'Anyway, why are you walking my path? The moon never warned me anyone was coming tonight.'

'Your path?' Dragonfoot queried, 'how do you own a path? And why do you nap in the middle of it?'

'Why not?' Moon Grá quipped. 'No one else treads this path, only me and my moths, so I've claimed it. As it's mine, I can nap wherever I choose. I certainly wasn't expecting to be trod on.' She spoke as she walked around him looking him up and down. As she did A little moth flew to her ear appearing to whisper something to her before planting a small kiss on her cheek. Then, flying around Dragonfoot's head once it flew away.

Moon Grá smiled. 'Ah, so you're the magic man who sent me a moth and a plant. The moon told me we'd meet at some point — thank you, I loved them both' she said winking with the last words. Dragonfoot blushed even more at this, in fact, it felt as though his cheeks were on fire! Suddenly Moon Grá noticed the red book poking out from one of his pockets and excitedly grabbed it.

'Oh, you have one — you must be a legend too!' She jumped with a squeal and began to flick through it. Dragonfoot a little embarrassed quietly said 'there's nothing written in it... yet.'

'Oh yes there is! Look!' Moon Grá spun the book around so Dragonfoot could see the pages and there on them were a beautiful array of letters! His belly felt all bubbly with excitement at the sight, Moon Grá quickly spun it back, skimming the pages as she spoke.

'Oh, you're like me, I don't really know where I came from either – Just appeared one day really. Hang on had you not realised it had started recording your quest? Don't get me wrong there are still blank pages but there really always will be until you... well erm... you know.'

Before he could answer she quickly pulled a blue book similar to his red one from behind a bush and shoved it in his hands.

'Look, here's mine – you can read it if you like. Mind you take some of the stories with a pinch of salt – I didn't actually ever eat the moon. In fact, it was the moon that dared me to fit it in my mouth - and it wasn't gone for days - in fact only for a few hours before I had to spit it out – the moths kept trying to fly in after it and that was not pleasant let me tell you!' She had gone off on a bit of a tangent, but Dragonfoot didn't mind as she spoke with such enthusiasm it was hard not to get whisked up in it too.

Dragonfoot sat down and got himself comfortable, getting ready to read some of her story. He looked in awe at the cover - a rich blue with silver writing on. 'The Legend of Moon Grá' it read. He traced his fingers over the script before opening it up. Her book seemed so jam packed, but he wasn't daunted by it. As he looked, he was pleased that the letters on the pages were becoming words easily in his mind - so there he sat and began to read happily.

'A full moon shone brightly in the clear
skies of Jadoo, there was magic
and mystery in the air. A cloud of
moths playfully chased the moon as
it wished as hard as it could for a
friend. People say this wish was heard
as it was that night the moths found a friend
for the moon. Her name was Moon Grá. She was a spritely
young thing with energy enough to play hide and seek with,
and she had no fear so the moths could fly her high in the
night sky to sing with the stars....

Moon Grá and Dragonfoot sat content reading silently, while
the moths fluttered around them every so often making an
attempt to touch the moon but never quite making it. Suddenly
Moon Grá looked up from the pages.

'What are you seeking?' she asked.

Dragonfoot hesitated, he didn't know really how to answer. 'Is
it not written in the book?' His reply sounded harsher than he
had intended.

It was Moon Grá's turn to blush, though hers seemed to be
more due to anger. She shut Dragonfoot's book loudly and,
whilst getting up to stand, handed it back to him.

'I was making conversation.' She snapped before adding 'and no, it does not. In fact, I'm not even sure you are seeking anything. I think you are wandering around at night-time treading on people.' Two large moths then flew either side of Moon Grá lifting her into the air before placing her gently on the highest branch of a nearby oak tree. Crossing her arms defiantly she turned away from Dragonfoot.

'I'm sorry!' Dragonfoot called as he walked over to the oak tree. 'I am seeking something, well in fact I'm seeking a couple of things.'

Though not meaning to, curiosity caused Moon Grá's head to turn slightly towards Dragonfoot.

'I seek the floating blue mountains!' he called louder. Dragonfoot had purposely not shouted out about the dragon's egg - he was worried who else may be listening.

'And??' Moon Grá called down from her branch having now fully turned to face Dragonfoot.

He stumbled a little both physically and verbally.

'Can you come down, so we don't have to shout?'

As he spoke, he felt his feet lift off the ground. Shocked he looked to his sides, right then left, and there they were - the two large moths - gently lifting him up to Moon Grá's branch.

Whispering she said, 'I'm sorry for my outburst, I speak so little to anyone but the moon and the moths I sometimes read people wrong as such.'

Dragonfoot quickly apologised too. 'No Moon Gr you are fine, I snapped a little not meaning to. Sorry.'

Apologies accepted, Moon Grá turned to Dragonfoot whispering 'What is the other thing you seek? It seems an important secret - it's probably safer to talk up here - well, if you don't mind the moon hearing. But it is good at keeping secrets' she added hurriedly, 'I should know it's kept all of mine.' With that she reached over and held Dragonfoot's hand.

'A dragon's egg, the last dragon's egg. And it's started to hatch.' His voice began to shake, Moon Grá squeezed his hand a little tighter – 'It's OK', she said 'we'll help you find it'.

In that moment he felt as though a weight had been lifted from his shoulders, he knew what she said was the whole truth – he trusted her, the moths and the moon. Squeezing her hand back he smiled a little – 'But how?'

Moon Grá jumped to her feet and then balanced on one leg throwing her other straight out behind her pointing to the moon 'The moon will look for you and, when it has found it, it will shine blue! But not your average blue – a blue so bright that it will make the jackalope sing and the songbird hop!' This made them both chuckle a little. Moon Grá then plopped herself back next to Dragonfoot.

'It's true' she said with a smile.

That night the two new friends shared plans and moon cakes. 'The moon and I will search for the, you know what, at night – so you, Dragonfoot, have to search during the daytime. OK?' Dragonfoot nodded, though he knew that this meant they would soon part ways. 'So, get some sleep,' Moon Grá advised gently showing him what looked like a large nest on one of the grand branches of the oak tree. 'This is where I nap when I don't feel like napping on the path,' she said with a little smirk. Dragonfoot did as he was told and curled up in the nest, it was lovely and warm and in no time, he was drifting off to sleep.

Chapter 12

Ready or Not

The morning light danced through the leaves, Dragonfoot
stretched and sat up. A note was perched on the branch. It
was from Moon Grá:

'The Moon and I have gone searching — we will send a
message if we are successful. Good luck on your quest and
keep safe! Remember to look out for the hopping songbird and
listen out for the jackalope's song!

PS. I saved you half my breakfast — enjoy!'

Sure enough, a half-eaten moon cake sat by the letter which
must have been written whilst she was eating as a few crumbs
littered the page. Though he missed his friend Dragonfoot was

filled with a hopefulness he hadn't felt before. Carefully he climbed down the tree and with a skip in his step he continued along the path.

He was not walking long before he heard the sound of a stream and remembered he had heard something similar when looking through his fallen stone at the dragon's egg. Excitedly he followed the sound off the path and into a wooded area. He was almost certain he'd find the egg in no time at all, and now, running through the trees, he suddenly came to a fast-flowing river. He couldn't help but feel a little disappointed that the dragon's egg wasn't right on the riverbank, but he decided to walk by the river keeping a beady eye out for any sign of the shimmering scaled egg.

As he walked, focusing on the flowing water, he was sure he sensed the trees moving – not just swaying in the breeze, as there seemed to be no such breeze today, but taking steps moving from one part of the ground to another. Every time Dragonfoot jerked his gaze to see them move he never caught them in the act.

Then suddenly with an almighty cracking sound and a thud, he finally saw a tree jump. It made him jump too, his hand quickly covering his mouth to mask the shocked scream that he was sure was coming.

Shaking the mass of leaves that was its head, the 'tree' leapt behind a rather small looking rock. As it crouched down, Dragonfoot heard it let out a stifled laugh.

'Coming ready or not,' called a small voice from deeper in the woods.

The owner of the voice soon emerged - a young woman, rather dramatically seeking high and low for the hider with no success. A small fairy fluttered by her.

'You only encourage him, Willow, when you play like this,' it grumpily said.

The woman, Willow, gently batted the fairy away. 'Shhh, he's only young and it makes him happy – what harm?' The fairy puffed out her chest.

'One day I warn you all, magic will no longer grace the worlds, he will be a static tree, and no one will see him. See if he likes it then. Hide and seek with a tree giant, goodness knows, it really is ridiculous.' She tutted and huffed the last part of her sentence.

Willow didn't pay her any attention and continued, 'Where can you be? I can't see you anywhere!'

Dragonfoot watched as she stood directly in front of the tree giant crouching behind the rock and couldn't help but smile.

She could clearly see him, and he was struggling to contain his laughter. The Fairy landed on him and stomped her foot shouting, 'He's here! Look! For goodness' sake!' before flying off back into the woods.

'Boo!' The tree giant suddenly leapt up from his hiding place – 'I win again!' he said triumphantly before running away calling behind him 'you're it again Willow!'

Willow put her hands to her eyes and started to count loudly, but before she could cover her eyes completely, she saw Dragonfoot.

'Hello,' she said, surprised to see him but not in any way scared.

'Eer, hello,' Dragonfoot replied with a small wave.

'Who or what are you?' The woman spoke softly, then realising her rudeness, introduced herself. 'Sorry, my name is Willow, I am an Earth Witch. The tree you saw running away is my friend, Arbre, a very young and playful tree giant. Did you also see the grumpy guts fairy?'

Dragonfoot nodded and Willow continued with a chuckle 'She's Ivy. She's not normally quite so grumpy - she's just a little upset at the moment. She's worried the magic will vanish somehow.' Shrugging, she held out her hand for a handshake.

Shaking Willow's hand, Dragonfoot asked, 'are you not worried?'

Willow shook her head, 'It's not possible. Magic will always grace the many worlds - even if not everyone can see it — some always will and so, magic will always be. So, you are?'

Dragonfoot had forgotten to answer her first questions, clearing his throat he spoke, 'I am called Dragonfoot, but to answer what I am, I don't really know myself. I seem to have started in the Beforan, but have no memory of being there, then I stayed with the Dragonfeet Tribe before...well...before bandits destroyed Draig Valley. Now I find myself here.'

Willow nodded slowly taking it all in, 'I can feel you are very magical, what can you do?'

Dragonfoot was happy with the change in topic as he felt himself tearing up a little. 'Well, I can change the colour of heather!'

'Oh, heather I like that name,' she said clapping her hands together with a broad smile 'what colours?'

'From white, to pink, to blues,' he said with a smile, thinking back to that day with Bea.

'What else can you do? Oh, can you change into a dragon? I've heard the Dragonfeet Tribe all could. Oh, I'd love to see that one day — I've never seen a dragon you know.' You could hear the excitement in Willow's voice as she asked these questions, but Dragonfoot couldn't help but start to feel upset. Not necessarily with the questions asked but with the answers that would follow.

'No,' he said slowly looking down at the ground, he didn't want to see the disappointment in her face. 'I can't change into a dragon, I'm not that magical a being.' Still looking down, he saw Willow's feet step closer to him. She bent down and placing her face in front of his looked up at him. Looking directly into his eyes she spoke with such certainty.

'Of course you are! We all have the ability to be *that* magical.'

Dragonfoot began to straighten up and Willow followed, continuing 'If you can change flowers to different colours what is stopping you changing, say, a rock to a feather or transforming yourself into a dragon? Don't let self-doubt dampen your magic. It may not happen today or tomorrow but one day you will see just how much magic you have in you.' She put her hands on his shoulders. 'Do you miss them? The Dragonfeet Tribe I mean.' Dragonfoot nodded. 'Are they what you are looking for?'

In that moment Dragonfoot wanted to tell Willow everything about what had happened so far and that yes, he was looking for the Dragonfeet Tribe but firstly he had to find the dragon's egg before it hatched. The urgency began bubbling inside him, but he didn't trust himself not to burst into tears and not being able to get out the words, so he just nodded again. Willow rubbed his shoulders gently before letting go, it looked like she was about to say something when a booming voice came from the woods.

'I'M READY!' Laughter followed. 'YOU'LL NEVER FIND ME!'

Willow chuckled, 'Well, Dragonfoot, it's lovely to have met you, but now I have a tree giant to find! Safe travels and no doubt we'll see each other again!' She headed in through the trees.

'COMING — READY OR NOT!' Dragonfoot heard her call as she went out of his view — he then continued on his way sticking close by the river.

Dragonfoot continued his journey. He loved the sound of the water and watching the tiny rainbow fish dancing in the ripples, though as he watched he thought he heard the faint sound of sniffing. Looking up he saw, Ivy, sitting on a branch just above the river. She held her knees close to her chest and Dragonfoot could see she was crying.

'Ivy?' He spoke gently trying not to alarm her. She turned to look at him as she wiped some tears away. 'Are you ok?' he asked.

Ivy shrugged and let her knees fall from her chest 'I'm not always so grumpy and I'm not a little worried – yes I heard Willow tell you – I am actually a lot worried.' She fluttered down to Dragonfoot 'You see, I've...' she flew to his ear and whispered 'I've lost a bit of my magic...'

Dragonfoot looked to her, 'How?' he asked, genuinely concerned for this tiny fairy.

'A key,' she sighed 'I had a key that allowed me to hop between worlds.' As she spoke, she showed Dragonfoot the tiny markings on her wings. They were similar to those on his leg. 'I was gifted this key, and it was my job to keep it safe and now I've lost it!' As the panic rose in her voice so did the volume 'It's my job to hop between the worlds and do...' she paused, realising she didn't really want to share all the fairy secrets with this stranger, '... magical things. But anyway, I have searched everywhere and I cannot find it. I'm in so much trouble.' She croaked the last few words before bursting into tears.

Dragonfoot mumbled, 'Is the key golden?' Her ears perked up and she looked directly at Dragonfoot 'Yes, yes, it is and it's about this big' she showed him with her hands.

Dragonfoot fumbled in his pockets as Ivy hopped and fluttered around him eagerly. After what seemed like ages, well to Ivy anyway who was an impatient little fairy, Dragonfoot produced a tiny golden key.

Ivy squealed with delight and scooped the key out of Dragonfoot's hands giving his finger a happy squeeze as she did so.

'Thank you! Thank you! Thank you!' She sang as she spun around excitedly. Dragonfoot chuckled as he watched her happy dance, and Ivy, realising his gaze, suddenly felt a little self– conscious and calmed herself.

'How does the key work?' Dragonfoot wondered out loud. He felt himself blush feeling Ivy would feel this question rude but to his relief she happily explained.

'Well, from one magic creature to another it's no harm you knowing – especially now it is back in my possession.' She flew up and gently landed on his hand.

'This key can open any portal to any world, – you just have to know where to find them. You see that tree over there?'

Dragonfoot looked at a beautiful silver birch standing proud and asked, 'Is that a portal?'

'No, no, not that one – that's a tree giant,' she tutted and shook her head, 'Can you imagine trying to open a portal on a tree giant – they'd sling you across the forest!' She laughed at the thought then continued 'behind that one.' Dragonfoot's gaze followed her outstretched arm and saw behind the silver birch tree giant was a large tree stump.

'That's the portal to my homeland,' said Ivy and with that she flew over to the stump, landing on the ground in front of it. Looking back to Dragonfoot she said, 'I hear the Dragonfeet Tribe are at the floating blue mountains and if that is what you seek you are in luck, they floated past us just this morning, you should find them in that direction,' she pointed down the river. 'Follow the river, you can't go wrong really as this is the only river that runs in Jadoo – You must hurry though and make it to the mountains before they reach the Forgetful Forest, if you fail there's no hope, you'll make it across – not this side of the year anyway!'

Yes, Dragonfoot did want to make it to the Floating Blue Mountains, but he knew he needed to find the dragon's egg first – and fast. Hearing Ivy say that this was the only river in Jadoo made his heart skip a beat The egg was near running water – if only he could be certain, it was still in Jadoo.

Dragonfoot was so distracted by the idea that the dragon's egg may be close by, he hadn't asked anything about the

Forgetful Forest. Ivy saw she was losing Dragonfoot to his thoughts as he wandered towards the river.

Calling as loud as she could she warned, 'Remember – try not to enter the Forgetful Forest, but if you do - do not fall asleep! Remember Dragonfoot!'

She watched him walk away and hoped he had heard her. She thought about flying after him to make sure, but her tummy grumbled, and she longed to get home. Shrugging, she convinced herself that he had heard, and she turned her key in the tree stump and vanished through the sparkling portal to her world leaving no trace behind.

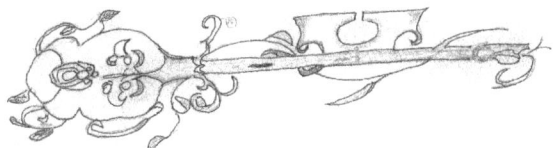

Chapter 12

The Jackalope's Song

Dragonfoot's ears twitched as he walked away from Ivy, he thought he had heard her call something - it must have been a goodbye and thank you. He'd mumbled a goodbye back and his eyes focused on the water as he hurried down to the riverside. He walked and walked but could see no egg, his heart began to feel heavy. As he walked, he thought about all the things he'd gone through to get here, all the people he'd met along the way — then one person stood out in his mind - Solas Grey. Dragonfoot remembered he had advised him to get on the floating mountains when he saw his chance and Ivy had told him they had been floating by here just today.

He hated to admit it, but he probably shouldn't miss his chance to get on the Floating Blue Mountains - maybe it was a sign. If he could get on them and find Bea, she could help him find the dragon's egg and hopefully before it's fully hatched. Dragonfoot despised the idea of it hatching all alone, he blamed himself, if only he could figure out where he sent it. All these thoughts were running through his head as he continued strolling by the water. He had not noticed the covering of trees he had walked into - so thick that they blocked out the blue skies. It was only when he heard the sound of snoring that he realised there were trees all around him - most being sleeping tree giants. A sweet smell filled the air.

Dragonfoot stepped slower and more carefully, looking around at where he was. It was a beautiful forest, he could see some pixies resting in the flowers. A little further in and he saw a minotaur snoozing against a tree stump – Dragonfoot was pleased that it was asleep as had heard what bad tempers they have. As he crept past the huge creature the thoughts of the dragon's egg and the floating mountains vanished from his mind, the sound of the snoring wasn't loud, in fact it was almost calming. His eyes began to feel heavy, but he continued walking, though slower still as he was unsure where he was walking to. Maybe he should sit down a while and try to remember. The ground was thick with moss, so soft under Dragonfoot as he plonked himself on the ground scratching his head.

'I know I am going somewhere, I know I am searching for something,' he spoke out loud trying to jog his memory. 'Where am I?' Looking around a thought popped into his head 'the Forgetful Forest' Willow and Ivy had spoken about this but what did they say about it. 'Remember Dragonfoot, remember!' He held his head in his hands. His eyelids were getting so heavy, the air so sweet, the sounds so soothing. He felt himself laying back onto the ground, as he did the Dreamseller's moonstone slipped from his pocket and fell to his side. He let his body sink into the cushion-like green moss, relaxed his arms to his sides, felt his eyes closing and his breathing slowing down as he began to drift off to sleep. The moonstone gently glided into his hand and began to glow.

A soft voice singing a familiar tune stirred Dragonfoot from his slumber, as his eyes opened, he saw he was no longer on a mossy ground but in a soft bed in a cosy room, a woody herbal scent filled the room and memories came flooding back to him - he knew this bed. Looking around he knew the room as well — he was at his home in The Beforan he recognised it all and the voice. He had to find the owner. Leaping out of bed he followed the tune out into the garden, a garden full to the brim with rosemary bushes, until there he found her. She was smaller than he remembered, more delicate almost, but her voice was the same. Silently he listened as he stood behind her, willing her to turn around yet nervous for when she would.

'Oh, sweet little child of mine, go travel the worlds.' Sang the voice then, to Dragonfoot's surprise, spoke 'Trust in yourself child'. She turned to face Dragonfoot. Her face he knew so well 'mum' he whispered. She smiled at him, a smile he had missed so much.

'But you shouldn't be here, not yet,' as she spoke, he felt the world around him changing. 'You are strong, brave, magical and above all kind. You are not seeking me or this place. Remember what you are seeking Dragonfoot.'

She embraced him as she spoke. He wished he could stay in her arms forever, but he could already feel her letting go. Behind her he saw the floating blue mountains and dragons flying high in the sky –their wings creating the dragon song and then he could swear he saw Ivy and Willow searching for Arbre; Solas Grey now with his hybrid pet; the tree keeper – all these faces were appearing around them as he struggled to keep focus on his mum. She slipped something in his pocket and whispered 'Rosemary – it helps you to remember,' then she pushed him hard, and he fell back. 'Now wake up!'

Landing with a thud his eyes shot open. He was on the moss, the snoring tree giants around him. Sitting up startled he saw the moonstone glowing in his hand – it had been a dream – but it seemed so real. He looked around him trying to remember what he was doing here, placing the moonstone back safely in his pocket he felt the sprig of rosemary – but how can that be?

The day having turned to dusk made the forest look different now, Dragonfoot saw the many creatures he had not seen before all in a state of sleep – it was peaceful, but he would not shake the feeling of urgency that had awoken him from his slumber.

Holding the rosemary in his hand he lifted it to his nose and breathed in, 'remember Dragonfoot, remember' he chanted to himself as he smelt the warm woody scent. A shimmering scaly dragon's egg came to the forefront of his mind – yes that is what he was looking for he must find it! Almost as soon as he remembered his mission the brightest moon you could ever imagine filled the night sky – but it did not shine a silvery hue tonight, no, it shone blue!

Dragonfoot's ears began to twitch as a song was carried in the light breeze 'a blue so bright it will make the jackalope sing and the songbird hop!'

Yes, he remembered it all! His eyes shot up to the sky and he saw a blue moonbeam pointing across the trees – guiding his way. He scrambled to his feet and ran as fast as he could, dodging the dozing creatures until finally, after what seemed forever, he was out of the trees - away from the snores – into the open clear night. It was only then that he noticed the water splashing around his feet. The moon's beam shone across the water to the land beyond -or did shine in the water? -, Dragonfoot struggled to see. He knew he would have to get closer but how. He had never swum before, he was unsure if he even could, but he knew he had to try - the dragon's egg needed him.

Looking across the water he watched the reflection of the stars dancing on the surface, he squinted trying to see where the blue moonbeam landed but still couldn't quite make it out at least, not for sure. Dragonfoot inhaled drawing the crisp night air into his lungs, filling them as much as he could, before he jumped into the cold clear water.

Chapter 14

The Last Dragon's Egg

The coldness stung his skin as he entered the water. The discomfort and unknowing made him scared, his dragon foot began to twitch and spark. Deeper he sank. The darkness surrounded him, and he could no longer see the blue light from the moon. He blinked, his eyes stung, his vision blurry. Then his lungs started to burn, he needed to take a breath. Kicking his legs frantically he desperately tried to swim to the surface, millions of sparks now flew from his clawed foot surrounding his body in dazzling light. It was then he felt a stretching feeling throughout his whole body, like something held his feet while another pulled his head. A sharp pain splintered through his muscles. He opened his mouth to scream, water flooded in, dulling the sound. Something swished below him and then it swished again, he began rising quickly through the water. Closing his eyes he lifted his head upwards; the speed he was going forced the water to break over his face it felt exhilarating. The swishing seemed to be getting faster and still just below him, he took his chance and looked down. To his surprise the water didn't sting his eyes anymore and his vision was crystal clear. Focusing on the depths just below him he saw a magnificent silver tail gliding through the water. It was his. He had transformed into the most wonderful silver, thing, but what was he?

Realising he could now breath freely under the water he began to wiggle his body around looking at all the different parts he had become. A long silvery tail, large, webbed feet and hands, his body slender like an eel yet his nose was now a snout like a dragon's! He let out an excited squeal and leapt out of the water into the night air before splashing back into the cold wet triumphantly.

Dragonfoot lost himself for a while as he darted this way and that and then diving even deeper into the bluey turquoise water. Many different sea creatures swam around him – deeper still he dove, taking everything in, feeling the excitement rising in him, then as he came to what he thought must be the bottom. He saw a strange structure ahead of him almost like a wall of coral.

The coral like structure was so tall Dragonfoot could not swim over it and although, if he were a little smaller, he could potentially squeeze through some of the gaps there didn't seem to be anything beyond the wall – just dark.

As he peered through the cracks he heard a scream of pain in the distance, he quickly turned to try and see if he could locate where it had come from and as he did a cloud of silt and bubbles appeared, moving towards him, getting closer and closer.

Suddenly a siren shot past Dragonfoot and through a gap in the coral wall, as it did, he saw a gash in its tail. It was obvious that this injury was due to a spear of some kind. As soon as the siren got past the wall a flash of blue lit the darkness. Dragonfoot watched in awe as he saw this light seem to heal the siren's tail and the pain vanished from its face.

The blue light made Dragonfoot remember why he was there, and he swiftly swam up to the surface searching for the moonbeam. It didn't take him long and he wasn't far from it. He followed the moon's sign - it directed him to the shore beyond. He swam faster and faster until he reached a sandy bank.

As he emerged from the water his silvery scales glistened in the moonlight. The breeze in the air dried his skin quickly and as it did, he felt himself return to his own skin. Dragonfoot took a couple more steps onto the shore and looked down at his feet, he was comforted to see his small foot and his dragonfoot had returned but was just as excited to have experienced what his magic could do. Glancing back across the water a glimmer of colour caught his eye. Without a second thought he ran over to it, almost falling over himself and there it was - no shadow of a doubt - the last Dragon's egg lay nestled in the mix of sand and grass.

Dragonfoot squealed with joy as he gently scooped the egg up, examining it carefully. There was the crack he had seen through his fallen stone but to his relief no others had appeared. He placed his ear to the eggs scales and listened. Yes, he could hear the dragon still moving around in the egg, and its heartbeat sounded steady., Dragonfoot embraced the egg as if it was a long-lost friend. Butterflies fluttered in his tummy, and he couldn't stop smiling. He was so happy it almost felt like he was floating! Then hearing dripping water, he looked down and could see, what looked like, a large blue cloud rising from the water and curling up around the land. It was then he was certain he was floating but not just him the whole island was rising up and up.

Tucking the dragon's egg safely in his bag made of leaves he scrambled up the bank a little more where he felt a safer, still hanging onto the ground with his clawed foot just in case he was to slip. As his foot gripped, he noticed the ground was a very light shade of blue and now, as he properly looked around him, he could see he was at the foot of an array of mountains - all different shades of blue — could it be — was he on the floating blue mountains? Yes, he was certain— the big giveaways were that the looming mountains were blue and were indeed floating!

After the initial fear of slipping had passed Dragonfoot began to enjoy being so high in the sky. He could see for miles and miles. Just below them was the large mass of water he'd explored and just beyond that was the Forgetful Forest - still full of snoozing plants and creatures. A small shudder passed through him when he thought that he may have been sleeping there still had it not been for the Dreamseller's moonstone and his mother's sprig of rosemary. Shaking his head to rid it of the thought he relaxed his dragon foot and began to think of where to go from here. The only way he really could go was up and so securing his bag on is back he began climbing up the surprisingly steep face of the mountain.

Chapter 15

Draig Falls

As he climbed, he began to think of Bea and the rest of the Dragonfeet Tribe. 'She'll be so pleased to see me' he thought 'and won't the elders be shocked that I've made it here.' His cheeks flushed a little with anger at that thought so he focussed on Bea. Dragonfoot didn't want or need any negativity – no, this was to be a happy moment, he would soon be reunited with his friend and then they could watch the dragon's egg hatch together.

When he felt like he could climb no more to his relief he found he had reached the top. Clambering up he sat for a moment to catch his breath. As he looked down the other side of the mountain he gasped with disbelief – he had never seen so many different magical beings in one place – what was this place? He began his descent slowly still trying to take in what he was seeing, why were there so many creatures here? Scanning the crowd, he looked for Bea, she must be here.

'You're new here' the voice came from above Dragonfoot, startling him. 'Don't worry you are both safe here.'.

Looking up, Dragonfoot could see an old woman sat on a cloud hovering by him. Her face was soft and friendly. Sensing he was unsure the woman stepped down from her cloud, she was very short so Dragonfoot had to look down. Noting his surprise, she laughed

'That's why I normally stay on my cloud!'

Dragonfoot couldn't help but let out a snort at her remark 'Laughter is just the best don't you think?' Pausing she clasped her hands together and looked one way then the next. 'I'll tell you what, let's summon you a cloud too and I'll show you around the place, hmmm?' Before Dragonfoot could really respond she was already conjuring up a cloud 'scamaill agus gaoth, scamaill agus gaoth, scamaill agus gaoth!' As she spoke the words a stone hung around her neck began to glow a deep teal. Suddenly a cloud appeared below Dragonfoot lifting him up into the air, unnervingly high, he doubted very much such a delicate thing could hold his and the eggs weight but to his delight it easily could. The woman climbed gracefully back onto hers and smiled again.

'My name is Varsha'

'Do you own this place? I mean run it?' Dragonfoot didn't really know what he meant and as soon as he asked the question, he felt it sounded silly.

'Oh no, no one can ever truly own a place as such. I have been here many, many years so I like to always make the newcomers feel welcome. There's no running here, unless you like to run for fun that is, but no rules - except to be kind.' Dragonfoot liked the sound of that.

'So, there are no,' lowering his voice to a whisper he continued 'bandits here?'

Varsha seemed a little shocked by this question. 'If they seek shelter and healing, they are welcome, but they are never doing wrong here, all that is washed away in the waters before they enter here. If it doesn't wash away then they cannot step foot, claw, hoof, fin or whatever on the mountain. The blue mountains are a safe space that creatures flock to in order to heal themselves, emotionally and physically, without the threat of being hunted.' Nodding to the dragon's egg she continued 'For example, your dragon can hatch here safely and stay for all it's years never needing to worry about bandits or wrong doers trying to catch it for its magical scales. Only here, on the blue mountains, will it be safe.'

Worried Dragonfoot asked 'Can no one ever leave?'

'Oh no, deary me, that's not what I meant. No, no! Many creatures can come and leave as much as they choose but dragons,' she paused and sighed 'I'm afraid to say, cannot – well, not safely anyway. They are by far the most magical of beings and, therefore, will always be hunted – in all the different worlds and universes. That is, except here.'

Dragonfoot sat silent for a while, taking in everything Varsha said. She did speak the truth, dragons are the most magical creatures and so they will never be safe to just live, but surely *having* to stay in one place wouldn't be that great either – not for such a grand creature that should be flying through the skies. Then another thing she said suddenly stuck out in his mind, 'are we not still in Jadoo here?' he asked. Varsha thought a little before answering 'Not really, no. The Floating Mountains are worlds in their own right like Jadoo and Draig and The Beforan BUT unlike those realms you don't need to be able to hop worlds or find portals in order to enter.'

She then clapped twice 'Come and let me show you around the mountain, there's lots to see and I have a sneaking suspicion you may recognise some creatures here. Come on, off we go!'

With that the clouds moved swiftly side by side as Dragonfoot looked around in wonder with butterflies replacing the worry in his tummy and his eyes looking out for Bea.

Dragonfoot had never seen so many shades of blue before, there were vibrant blue poppies scattered over the mountainside and then soft blue clouds hugging the higher peaks. As they got to the south side Dragonfoot's ears twitched - he could hear the sound of water thundering down, it was almost too loud, rubbing his ears Varsha called over to him 'This is Draig Falls, the sound can be overwhelming to begin with but if you focus on the falling water, it almost becomes melodic. I had heard it was similar to that of the Dragon's song.'

Dragonfoot looked over to the turquoise blue waters running over the rocks and crashing down into the plunge pool below. Focusing on the movement he did begin to hear the Dragon's song, his heart jumped, then beyond the Dragon's song he heard that of laughter and softer splashes. Instinctively he moved his body forward and down, the cloud responded, taking him away from Varsha and down to the rocks at the bottom of the waterfall. Watching, Varsha, stayed a little a way leaving Dragonfoot to find the laughter on his own, she felt he would've wanted that.

Hearing the laughter again but louder, Dragonfoot, knew he was close by to its owner. He stepped off the cloud, slipping a little on the wet rocks, then steadying himself he walked closer to the plunge pool and peered in. The sight that met him made him almost fall in! There, splashing and giggling like hatchlings were nine of the ten Dragonfeet Tribe elders! Dragonfoot clutched his mouth to stifle a laugh that was coming, then before he knew what was happening, he was being lifted in the air and thrown into the water. He made a big splash as he entered the cool blue waters, then immediately after an even bigger splash happened, as the tenth elder canon balled in. Spluttering and laughing Dragonfoot began to tread the water, bobbing up and down he turned to face all the elders. 'We're very happy to see you child,' they said almost in unison – this made Dragonfoot's heart fill up. 'And look,' one spoke as he pointed to Dragonfoot's back, 'he has the dragon's egg safely with him!' Swimming to face Dragonfoot and gently placing his hand on his shoulder the elder continued, 'Bea knew you would.'

At this Dragonfoot's eyes lit up, the elders chuckled. One nodded his head to the other side of the plunge pool. Dragonfoot followed the nod until his eyes fell upon a figure on the side, a broad smile and glasses shimmering in the sun. BEA!

Dragonfoot swam as quickly as he could to her and clambering out of the water embraced her immediately. She hugged him just as hard back.

'You made it!' She spoke, almost in a whisper. 'I knew you would.'

She pulled away from the embrace and held his shoulders, looking deep in his eyes, Dragonfoot could see tears were starting to fill them, then wiping her eyes she chuckled 'You've even grown a little too!'

He smiled at her comment, especially as she still towered over him. 'It must be all the magic in me that's making me taller,' he told her in jest but also with a little bit of pride.

Bea smiled her broad smile then, clapping her hands together in excitement she started to pull Dragonfoot towards a small opening in the waterfall.

'Look here,' she pointed inside. 'I have made the egg a perfect place for it to hatch.'

Dragonfoot peered into the opening and saw the gold and gems that covered the floor and walls, yes, the dragon would be very happy hatching here, but he couldn't help but have a sinking feeling in his tummy. Something was not sitting right with him, he wasn't sure the dragon would be happy here, not truly, not forever. Although Bea had noticed his look, she chose to ignore it and reached for the egg from his back.

'Look it fits perfectly,' she said as she placed it gently down. Suddenly she noticed the crack. 'Oh, it's already hatching!' She said a little shocked.

'Yes, that's why I got to safety so quickly' Dragonfoot snapped, then blushed, 'sorry, I just, I am just not sure about all of this.' He spluttered, scooping the egg up and walking away from Bea.

He walked all over the mountains, from Draig Falls to the Midnight peaks. As he walked, he saw so many different creatures all seemingly happy, but he also noticed that he saw very few homes, in fact the only 'homes' he remembered glimpsing was that of the Dragonfeet Tribe. Dragonfoot remembered Varsha saying that everyone was free to come and go as they please, but he couldn't shake the feeling of dread when thinking this dragon would *have* to stay here, for its own safety she had explained. But still, it didn't sit well with Dragonfoot. Dusk had drawn in by the time he reached the top of Midnight Peaks, and the moon was creeping high in the sky, not quite as full but it shone enough for Dragonfoot to see all across the floating mountains. He watched as creatures departed, vanishing in the waters and the skies, returning to their homes and adventures yet to come.

'Why do I feel so low?' he asked the sky, 'surely the waters should have washed away my sadness and doubt and I should be happy like everyone else?' he spoke clearly but was not expecting an answer so as one came just a clear back it startled him a little.

'The feelings you are feeling are not bad, the waters wash away any need to act on badness, but feelings can still be felt — they should be felt.' It was Bea, she'd come to find him when he had gone for so long. She sat down next to him and placed her hand on his, 'I can see you're not happy to stay here,' pausing a little before continuing 'I can also see you don't want to leave the dragon's egg, you have bonded so much with it — that is clear to see — but,' she paused again, for longer this time, trying to figure out how she was going to continue. 'Dragonfoot, you have seen how the worlds will hunt this egg as it is now and continue even after it hatches. It will be too big for some worlds, too magical for others and in some it will be wanted for its skin, teeth, horns, claws, wings and head! Here it will be safe.'

Dragonfoot looked at Bea, 'But this is not the type of living this dragon wants, I can feel it, it wants to fly the skies and experience the different worlds. I know I sound crazy, but I truly believe this and I think I know a way I can make it happen.'

Bea took a deep breath in, yes, she fully thought Dragonfoot was speaking nonsense, and she wanted to argue her point, but the serious behind his eyes, the determination, kept her silent. She squeezed his hand, 'I believe you,' she spoke as she stood up and started to walk back down the mountainside.

Dragonfoot watched until she went out of sight, then looked back up to the moon briefly before looking down to the egg that safely on his lap and there perched so delicately on it was a moth. It had been drawn to the moon's glow reflecting off the egg's scales, Dragonfoot watched it, it seemed so content walking about the egg then after a little rest it then spread its wings and off it flew into the night sky. Dragonfoot's eyes suddenly filled with hope and excitement — yes — he knew exactly what to do!

Chapter 16

Snathaid Mhor

The next morning Dragonfoot had a spring in his step. He almost skipped to Draig Falls, with the Dragon's egg in his arms on full display. When he reached the waterfall, he found all the Dragonfeet Tribe splashing and playing in the plunge pool, scanning the pool and the banks for Bea he could barely hide his excitement. Finally, he saw her, as he caught her eye, he waved so frantically he almost dropped the egg! Bea chuckled at this and ran around to greet him. They hugged each other then Dragonfoot grabbed her hand,

'Come with me,' he was so happy he skipped and hopped as he led her up the side of the waterfall and to a calmer part of the river, then placing the egg carefully down on the grassy bank he gestured for Bea to sit down by it. She sat down, still confused but bemused by the giddiness of Dragonfoot.

'I know exactly what I must do for this dragon,' he said while kneeling in front of the egg, placing both his hands gently on it. He then turned to Bea, his hands still on the egg and said, 'things change and can change so suddenly, just think of Draig Valley how quickly it went from a safe haven to a danger zone, who knows - the blue floating mountains may not float one day and where would that leave the dragon?'

Bea was not sure where Dragonfoot was going with this but still he continued. 'Trust me Bea, I know how to make this dragon live happily and free.' Barely stopping to breathe Dragonfoot looked back to the egg and his foot began to twitch. As sparks began to fly from it, so his hand also began to spark. Bea was nervous, she began to fidget, then the egg began to glow. Dragonfoot began to sing, starting almost as a whisper, '*libellule, gwas y neidr, libelle,*' he began to get louder as the egg became brighter and brighter, Bea had to shield her eyes, '*snathaid mhor,* dragonfly!'

He almost shouted the last word as the egg shattered under his hands. Bea gasped, her hand covering her mouth in shock, then suddenly she saw the most beautiful thing –the sky became full of small, long creatures she had never seen before, they were so many different colours and had such delicate wings.

'They are Dragonflies,' Dragonfoot proudly said, 'free to roam in any of the worlds. As no one would suspect such delicate, small, creatures would hold such magic as that of a dragon' He smiled, and Bea smiled back at him as she watched the dragonflies fluttering all around them. The cluster of colourful insects began to disband as they flew in all different directions off into the world, except one that had perched on Dragonfoot's shoulder.

'You clever, clever, little Dragonfoot,' Bea spoke with such pride. She clasped his hands in hers, 'such a magical being! I knew you were special when I found you in that bush.' She sighed a happy sigh, 'I am so proud of you.'

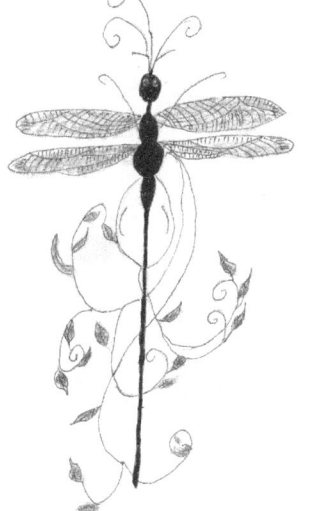

Dragonfoot's tummy fizzed with happiness, the sinking feeling had gone, he knew he had done the right thing, and he was proud of himself too. Happily, the two friends got up, the shattered shell of the dragon's egg had vanished into the ground until there was almost no sign of it.

Suddenly Bea grabbed tight onto Dragonfoot's hand and did a running jump off the waterfall! Dragonfoot screamed, which soon turned into a squeal as they landed with a big splash at the bottom. There the two played happily with the rest of the Dragonfeet Tribe for most of the rest of the day.

Afterwards Bea showed him her new inventions - one being something she called a post box — 'so if someone isn't home when you call you can leave them a note' she had proudly said. Dragonfoot loved how she was able to still be so creative — being here really suited Bea.

That evening as they sat by a campfire Dragonfoot told of his adventures through Jadoo; the Crossroads; the Forgetful Forest and the scuffle he had with the bandits. All the Tribe listened, laughed and gasped in all the right places. Dragonfoot wondered if this is how the Storyteller feels when he tells his tales. He thought about this for a while, he would like to see the Storyteller again, in fact he'd like to meet up with all his friends again. The night drew in and the Dragonfeet Tribe all retired to their caves, Dragonfoot, however opted to stay by the campfire for the night, he found the night sky comforting — tonight especially so as the skies were so clear you could see millions and millions of stars!

When he knew he was on his own he took off his belt bag and emptied its pockets, smiling as he did so. The moonstone from the Dreamseller had let him see his mother again, the silver tongue from the Storyteller had saved his life when the Goddesses of the Crossroads demanded a gift, and then there was his book from the Bookworm — now brimming with words but still a fair few blank pages — Dragonfoot liked this, it showed to him he had many more adventures to go on.

The final item he pulled out was the fallen stone. He held it in his hand and smiled, it was such an ordinary looking thing, yet it held the key to seeing all the different worlds and universes, he held it to his eyes and muttered the word 'adventure' it sparked to life and flashing through the holes were worlds upon worlds each more colourful and interesting. Dragonfoot smiled as he closed his hand around the stone, then placing all the items back in his belt bag he placed it on, stood up and walked to edge of the floating world diving in as his dragonfly friend hovered over the water's surface.

The next morning Bea woke up extra early and ran out to see Dragonfoot, but he was no longer by the fire that was now just a few embers as she walked up to the stone seats that circled it, she knew that he had gone. There on one of the stones written in charcoal was a note for her 'I will be back again one day but until then I will write to you. Love DF.' Bea couldn't help but feel a little sad but she knew he had to go and she couldn't wait to receive a letter from him. Luckily for her she didn't have to wait long....

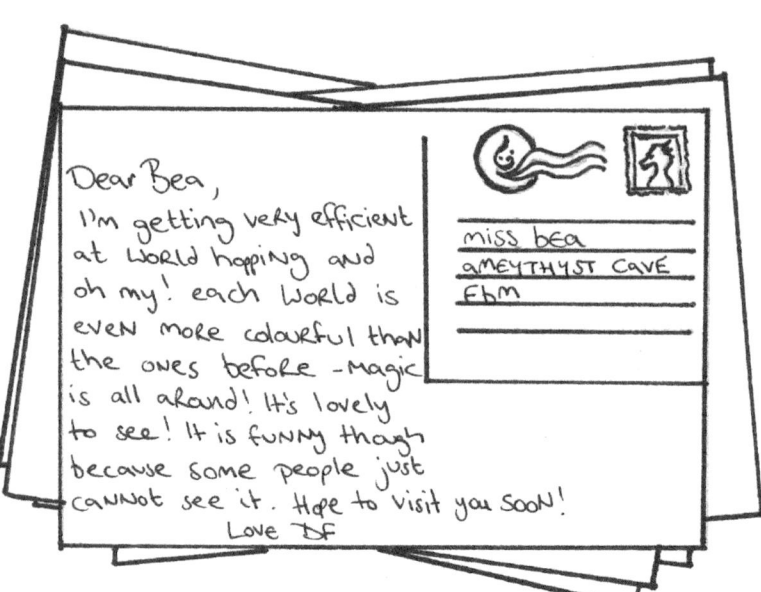

Dear Bea,
I'm getting very efficient
at world hopping and
oh my! each world is
even more colourful than
the ones before - magic
is all around! It's lovely
to see! It is funny though
because some people just
cannot see it. Hope to visit you soon!
Love DF

miss bea
aMEYTHYST CavE
Fbm

Glossary of the Characters:

Name: Bea, of the Dragonfeet Tribe

Origin: Draig Valley

Magical Powers: Like all members of the Dragonfeet Tribe, Bea can transform into a magnificent dragon-like creature, summoning the magic of the earth with a powerful stomp of her clawed feet. When she soars through the skies, embers of ancient energy shimmer in her wake. She also possesses the curious ability to shift the colours of plants at will—a trick dismissed by the grumpy Elders as mere mischief.

Favourite Things: Amethysts shimmer with the same deep magic that hums beneath her feet, making them her most treasured gems — plus she adores the colour purple! She loves finding and inventing new things - finding joy in crafting clever creations—her enchanted glasses sharpen her sight, while her belt bag holds more secrets than it seems.

Name: Dragonfoot

Origin: The Beforan

Magical Powers: A traveller between realms, Dragonfoot can 'hop' between all the many magical worlds, vanishing in a heartbeat and reappearing wherever the unseen threads of the cosmos allow. It is said he was born with this gift, though years of rigorous training have sharpened his abilities. Now, few can match the grace and precision with which he moves between realities.

Favourite Things: Adventure calls to him like a distant drumbeat, and he answers without hesitation. He delights in uncovering strange and wondrous stones, each one a fragment of a story waiting to be told. The colour red sets his spirit alight, as fiery and bold as his journeys. And after a long trek, nothing pleases him more than a warm, crumbly rock cake—preferably one fresh from the fire.

Name: Dreamseller

Origin: The Realm of Midnight Skies

Magical Powers: As their name suggests, the Dreamseller deals in dreams, woven from moonlight and captured in glowing moonstones. These coveted treasures are usually bought with gold, but sometimes—when the stars align and the wind hums with longing—they are found wandering beneath the night sky, appearing only when a dream is truly needed.

Favourite Things: While gold holds a certain gleam, their heart belongs to the hush of night. They revel in the stillness when the world is quiet, when dreams take shape beneath the stars, and the only sound is the whisper of the wind carrying forgotten wishes.

Name: The Goddesses of the Crossroads

Origin: True origin unknown but some say a land called Greece in a magical world known as Earth

Magical Powers: These enigmatic beings exist between realms, weaving the fates of those who pass through their domain. Appearing at crossroads, where destiny wavers, they bestow fortune or misfortune upon travellers, guided only by the offerings they receive. A simple token might bring luck, while an ill-chosen gift could summon ruin.

Favourite Things: Though their many heads bicker and banter, they all share a single love—gifts, gifts, and more gifts! The shinier, the better. Trinkets of gold, silver, and gemstones catch their many eyes, and they hoard their treasures with the delight of dragons.

Name: Maximus, the Tree Nymph

Origin: The Oak Tree, Beyond Draig Valley

Magical Powers: Lacking magic of his own, Maximus instead carries a rare and wondrous treasure—a fallen stone, a hole naturally pierced straight through it. Through this enchanted hole, he can glimpse hidden worlds, magical realms that remain unseen to others.

Favourite Things: Few things please him more than the sound of his own voice, spinning tales about himself with the enthusiasm of a bard who never tires. His second greatest love is his fallen stone, the key to a thousand unseen worlds—though whether he loves it more than talking about it remains a mystery.

Name: Moon Grá

Origin: She was woven from starlight

Magical Powers: A celestial spirit, Moon Grá dances among the stars, her laughter rippling through the night sky. She speaks in whispers to the moon and hums lullabies to the moths, her presence a mystery that lingers long after she drifts away on the silver wind.

Favourite Things: She drifts in the glow of the moon, whispers secrets to the moths, and twirls beneath the twinkling stars. But her greatest joy is the moment a shooting star streaks across the sky—brief, brilliant, and full of unspoken magic.

Name: Solas Grey

Origin: The Sunny Plains, Jadoo

Magical Powers: Though he possesses no true magic, Solas Grey walks the world as if it bends to his charm. His easy confidence and boundless warmth open doors where others find only walls, leading him to places even the most powerful sorcerers cannot reach. While his luck sometimes falters, his ever-present smile never does. Ever chasing the sun, he moves with the golden glow of adventure, as if the light itself guides his path.

Favourite Things: His most cherished companions are his two magnificent hybrid pets, dazzling creatures with peacock heads, lion bodies, and serpent tails. With three mismatched feet—one an elephant's, another a deer's, and the third a tiger's—they are as peculiar as they are enchanting, and he never misses an opportunity to parade them before an awestruck crowd.

Name: Storyteller

Origin: Jadoo

Magical Powers: His voice does more than tell tales—it conjures them into existence. As he speaks, the visions of his stories rise from his very eyes, shimmering and shifting like living dreams, wrapping his listeners in a world spun from pure magic.

Favourite Things: Wherever he goes, his two loyal lurchers follow, their silent presence a steady comfort as he weaves his tales. They are his constant companions, listening with knowing eyes as his magic spins stories into the air.

Now it's time to add yourself to this magical tale...

Name:

Origin:

Magical Powers:

Favourite Things:

Glossary of Words:

Beforan — Old English for 'in former times'

Draig — Welsh for 'Dragon'

Gwas y neidr — Welsh for 'Dragonfly'

Jadoo — Hindi for 'Magic'

Libelle — German for 'Dragonfly'

Libellule — French for 'Dragonfly'

Scamaill agus gaoth — Irish/Gailge for 'Cloud and wind'

Snathaid Mhor — Irish/Gailge for 'Dragonfly'

Did you know... every year, scientists uncover new species of animals, beetles, trees, and more — proof that our world is still brimming with wonders waiting to be discovered.

www.ingramcontent.com/pod-product-compliance
Ingram Content Group UK Ltd.
Pitfield, Milton Keynes, MK11 3LW, UK
UKHW050423030725
460357UK00004B/19